I Made It Out

By The Grace of God

Lawrence C. Boles III

Published by CaryPress Publishing

www.carypress.com

ISBN-13: 978-1-63103-030-7

DEDICATION

I want to dedicate this book to everyone who supported me when I felt so undeserving. In my darkest hour where I had given up on life, you were right there to hold me up. Your prayers for me, with me and your love and encouragement have left me in awe of all of you. Thank you Mom, Linda Winston you are the greatest ever! Thank you grandma and granddad, Lemmie & Ora Winston. To all of my sisters LaSundra M. Winston, Salaythiea O. Boles, Jammie L. Hampton, Christiana M. Hampton and to my entire church family, Redeemed By The Blood Pentecostal Church of God in Christ. I love you all so much. It's because of your love, support and showing me the true meaning of family that gave me the hope I needed to live again. Know that this is only the beginning!! And to my dad and all my children know that I love you.

A special thank you and shout out to a creative mind and a friend that I've grown to know through this experience of writing my book, what an amazing opportunity God has allowed for us to partner together in such a successful endeavor. Thank you Reishon professionally known as Staxx Cordero, for your support and believing in me and pushing me to fulfill my dreams and expressing myself in a different way in and reaching the masses beyond the pulpit! Looking forward to creating many more books. Thank you sister Felicia Foster for the recommendation. I'd also like to thank James Jacobs for all of your amazing creativity and your patience in designing my book cover and fliers and all the long nights in preparing for this special day.

Last but not the least, to the very breath of my Life, my best friend, my companion, my wife Jacqualine Savanna Boles, you are the greatest, and not only do you share the dedication of this book, but I dedicate the very success of my life to our relationship and to the pure love that I have for you and our family. If not for the love that you have shown me this would have never been possible. I thank you for loving me back to life and accepting me in spite of my past, I'm grateful for you. I'm so happy that you didn't allow what people said about me interfere with what God had promised for us. *I Love You* Jacqualine Savanna Boles, better known as (Sweets.)

I Made It Out By The Grace of God

CONTENTS

FOREWORD

My desire and motivation to compose this book was because I knew that my story was not intended to be kept quiet. It was supposed to be shared to a broader audience to hopefully help and to inspire you to continue on, in spite of your past. My desire is to remind one that your promise is much greater than your previous or present predicament. It's not about *where you are*, but *where you're going*. And believe it or not, we are all purposed with destiny, and we can't die until we fulfill the promise. So, in spite of the level or intensity of your story or testimony don't let that stop you from change. Because if God can do it through me, then he's faithful enough and more than able to do it through you.

Team Redeemed
Pastor Lawrence Christopher Boles III

1 CHAPTER ONE

S tanding in front of the mirror, slipping into my robe I admired my reflection. I'm far from perfect but I can see where God has molded and renewed me. God is first, and my wife is my best friend and confidante. My family is a priority and feeding the souls of the congregation is my passion. I do not take my responsibilities lightly, it is truly an honor and extreme blessing to be in this position.

As I reviewed my sermon I could hear the church filling up and I turned to the monitors to check on my beautiful wife Jacqueline. She is my rock and is always in tune with me spiritually. Watching my wife with pride I see her speak with the music director and choir lead. I am completely appreciative of us in this path together, as she addresses the congregation I raise the volume on the monitor allowing her voice to fill my office. As my wife Jacqueline led praise and worship, I felt the all too familiar embrace as the holy spirit filled me.

Tears filled my eyes with gratitude and I fell to my knees crying with joy that I have been made anew. I was now loved and adored for all the right reasons. Hearing the choir singing Darwin Hobbs' *"He's able,"* and the congregation roaring with praise, I identified with them as I was just as overjoyed at that very moment. I could hear them crying, and shouting their praise for being in church on this joy filled Sunday morning. Although I am of the cloth, I too am grateful for the wake up and did my praise dance in the form of a two-step in my office. I'd never be too cool to praise the Lord for all he does and all he allows me to be.

Who are we to question the Lord... but I'm human and so many questions fill my mind as to how I could be deserving of such a complete 360 turn around in my life. Who I am and who I've become are truly a part of my testimony. It all makes sense for all I've seen and countless situations in which I've played a key role. My leadership skills were never in question but *who* I led at different times in my life was questionable. It warmed my heart to see many of whom I interacted with in my past life take a new walk in faith. Too many times I'd see some of the brothers and sisters from my past consider coming to church and even give me a pound on it but never show. But when they do show up they're so touched by the sermon some of them take the walk to the altar and join me on one of my greatest roles of leadership as a Pastor.

I am grateful for everyone that comes to the altar to accept Christ as their Lord and Savior but a different kind of gratitude filled my heart when a former gang member joins the church. It lets me know that my words touched them to the core and they couldn't ignore the pull of God wanting to lead their lives in a new direction. I recognized the pain in their eyes of lost family members, of not knowing what tomorrow holds I understood pending sentences, time served, threats on their lives, bodily harm, lives taken, lives they've taken, countless fights and never telling because your word was everything. Knowing that I'm not so far removed, whenever a gang member comes to the altar it only increases my faith.

I grew up in church as far as I can remember we were in church every Sunday without fail. From 9:45AM-3PM we could be found in Bethany Temple Pentecostal Church. I'd be dressed up in a button up shirt, tie, slacks and shoes. Of course being a kid I'd be distracted and not hear the whole sermon delivered by my uncle, Pastor Willie Calloway. But my eyes would pop open when he became animated and screamed out certain parts of the sermon, when he began sweating and his eyes bulged for emphasis. One of my favorites "oh ya'll ain't with me this morning?" That always made the congregation come alive as they competed for whom the word touched the most. He'd mop his brow and continue the sermon. He had a way with the congregation and they were faithful to him. Every Sunday those seats were filled, everyone in my household definitely had a permanent seat.

I didn't know how much of his style I took with me but looking back, my uncle Willie was more instrumental in who I've become than I could have ever imagined. Every Sunday without fail after church everyone would gather at my house with trays of food and the children would play in the backyard. Our games were limited come to think of it but no different than who I am today... if we played house, I was the dad. If we played church I was the pastor. I mocked my uncle's mannerism and improvised my version of what he preached that day. I'd set up the chairs with a section for the congregation, a section for the choir and I positioned the lawn chair to face everyone. I'd detach the microphone from the record player and we'd play until we were called in for dinner.

There were about eight of us and we all played two or more roles, congregation, choir and one of us had to play my uncle Theto and aunt Bey when they praised. Aunt Bey always bent over backwards during her praise. All the kids always searched for one another in church when she got up to praise we smiled hard knowing we'd imitate her later. Those were some of the greatest moments of mine as a kid. I was fascinated by the reaction to my uncle's sermon every Sunday and I loved the way the choir sung.

I was also fascinated with the different areas I saw when I rode the bus from Skyway (Seattle) through the CD (Central District.) Intrigued and with admiration the older dudes who looked cool sagging their pants, the white Air Force Ones, the shiny cars with gold rims. I'd see them counting their money out in the open for anyone to see, they had swag and I wanted to have that. I wanted money of my own to count, I needed to know how to be down with them the guys from "Deuce 8," they were doing it!

Now don't get it twisted my family had money. They worked hard and had careers, had rental property, and drove nice cars. We lived in the suburbs, where I saw none of the guys from Deuce 8 aside from this bus ride. There was an itch in me that could not be contained, I *wanted* to be a part of the hood. I found myself doing research on it, asking questions only to find out that my cousins (by marriage) the Jamison's actually started "Deuce 8."

In 5th grade I got a taste of life as a BGD (Black Gangster Disciple) and there was no turning me back. I was always curious about what the process would be to be down and here I was about to find out! I was about to be initiated to be a BGD, in order to be down I had to make it through 6 people. Three on either side and if I fell on the floor I had to start over. I fought everybody including the person at the end. It was 12 minutes of fighting! I was exhausted but I never hit the floor because I was determined to prove myself worthy of being a BGD. I was in! I was kind of sore fighting 6 dudes but it was worth it. I was down now!

I was moving like a "g," doing what I wanted, when I wanted and no one could stop me. I was skipping school here and there hanging out drinking Mad

Dog 20/20 and Old English 22's. Since we couldn't get our hands on any bamboo paper, we used to smoke weed and made pipes out of aluminum. We spent our time hanging out on the bridge which led to the Skyway Park, a desolate area where we could see the police before they saw us. We were up there shooting dice, breakdancing, getting high and freestyling. I wasn't thinking about missing school or the impact it may have had on my future and decision making. I was living it up.

It was rare that I went to school but when I did there was a kid in class that got on my last nerves! Ol goofy Ralph, he was as tall as can be for no apparent reason. He always looked like he was lost or he made the silent fart that made the class sick to their stomachs I couldn't stand him! If we played ball I could count on losing with him on my team because he had butterfingers with the pass and never and I mean *never* made the basket! I used to mess with him all the time and one afternoon my teacher Mr. Lockhart couldn't take it anymore so he decided me and goofy could have a one on one right in the class. He dismissed the class a few minutes early and we stayed behind. He moved the desks and chairs out of the way to allow space for us to fight. The kids that were dismissed were in the hallway pushing and shoving each other out of the way in efforts to see the fight through the classroom window.

I guess Mr. Lockhart thought that kid had it in him to teach me something. He and Goofy could pass for family as they both had the matching flat tops. Mr. Lockhart made himself comfortable on his desk, partially sitting on the desk with one leg hanging off. I was excited, this is what I do! An uninterrupted fight where I didn't get into trouble? Let's rock! BGD representative right here! Mr. Lockhart was tired of me fighting and picking on the kids and I was tired of him calling my house and complaining to my parents. When Mr. Lockhart gave the head nod for us to fight I wasted no time.

The inner beast within me escaped and I whipped goofy Ralph from one side of the class to the other. I took the fight as gym time and we got it in a good five minutes. I think he may have gotten in a hit or two but that's it. I lumped him up and had a good time doing it. The whipping was justified because I couldn't stand him. Those free five minutes of fighting were supposed to do *what*? I wore him out and I learned nothing. I still bullied people, causing havoc, and chaos every time I entered the school.

Although I checked out mentally from school they still tried their best to keep my interest. One of the teachers went out of his way to help me, Mr. Maccabee. He used to try to encourage me to do my homework. It was one of the key reasons I was failing aside from not attending or participating. I wasn't doing the homework. It's not that I couldn't do the work, I wasn't interested. But good old Mr. Maccabee would come to my grandparents' house and try to tutor me.

My grandmother was the ultimate housewife. She was always home, ready to prepare grilled cheese sandwiches and some iced tea. It was cool but I still wasn't encouraged to do my work. Eating my grilled cheese sandwich I showed off my manipulation skills by having him do the work for me. I had no intentions of doing any homework he was completely wasting his time. Anything that required me to think was laughable. I'd find a way for him to lead me to the answer and he fell for it every time. I acted like I couldn't come up with the answer on my own, he felt like he helped me but I was just passing the time, enjoying my homemade grilled cheese sandwich.

In 6th grade I started skipping school on a more regular basis. And when I was there you could count on finding me in the principal's' office. I was definitely a menace in school, entertaining the kids that wanted to see a fight. I was feared by the boys who thought they were my next victim and a headache to my teachers when I was there. Since I spent most of my time in the principal's office, I found more ways to get into trouble. I'd become a thief! I'd steal from the principal office. The principal would leave me in the office and threaten to call my house. My retaliation for all these phone calls and detention was stealing.

With too much time on my hands, I was snooping around and found the drawer where all the goodies were. I confiscated everything from the principal's office that was confiscated from the students. I took, flip phones, cameras, beepers, yoyo's, dice, fat shoe strings, bandanas and I was selling it back to the kids at a higher price or the same price than they originally paid. I didn't bring the items to school unless they brought the money. The kids were in awe that I could get my hands on it. They all wanted to know how I was taking their belongings and the principal didn't figure it out until my grandfather made me admit what I was doing. I hid all my findings in a big bush right outside my grandparents house. My grandfather knew I was up to something but he couldn't figure out what it was.

One day he just happened to be at the window as I walked up the block from school. He hid in a corner peeping from the curtain, spying on me from the window and saw me make my daily drop. I came into the house like I normally do and he stopped me dead in my tracks. He had the belt ready to go! I got the same type of whipping that I gave goofy Ralph! Grandpa whipped me from one end of the living room to the other. I ran out of the house when he allowed me to and I gathered all the stuff I'd been taking. I turned it all in to the principal the next day who was just about done with me. She just looked at me in disbelief but that expression would be one I'd grow accustomed to in the years to come.

2 CHAPTER TWO

Jeremiah 29:11 - For I know the plans I have for you,"

I n my skipping school I started terrorizing dudes at other schools that were in different gangs. I was feared because of my skills. They knew the beat down was coming if I was in close proximity. Constantly recognized for my handiwork I was nice with the fists and would lay you out if you tried me. After one fight where I laid this dude out I was recognized by a member of Deuce 8! I heard him but I played it cool when he said, "that's deuce 8 right there." I wanted to scream and jump in the air but I waited for them to approach me because I didn't want to appear too eager.

Getting that nod of approval from Deuce 8 made me act out event more! I felt unstoppable and powerful.

It was definitely a boost of confidence for me. It felt me feel invincible I was feeling like Jordan right now! This initiation was different though. Instead of being "jumped in," you fought someone that matched your ability in efforts to make you a better fighter. I handled my fight like a champ even though I didn't win, it excited me to learn a new fighting style. Being a part of Deuce 8 had me so hype. I felt like I was that dude! I was fighting a lot though, continuously sharpening my skills. I hid my scars from my mother and grandmother by wearing a hoodie and staying in my room. If someone saw a scar I'd brush it off or lie and say I had a fight or I'd gotten jumped.

As the teen years approached I found myself testing the waters and no one was exempt. I was fighting in school constantly and probably starting my mom's grey hair early. She was trying to save me from my own destructive behavior but I was uncontrollable. I started skipping school and hanging out in the hood all day and all night. I'd walk from Deuce 8 down to the Space Needle. There was no question of where I'd been until the police picked me up and detained me over night, they would bring me into the school and someone in the office would contact my mother. This scare was temporary, a few days later I'd be back in the hood skipping school again.

I was more than a handful for my mom as she passed me to different family members in an attempt to get a handle on me. I'd been through at least five schools with the same results, I refused to go. My teachers had no idea of who I was, my education was coming from the hood. I was more into learning about street life than what any textbook could teach me. I wasn't afraid to be out there, I wanted to be out there.

With my face becoming familiar, I started selling crack and smoking weed. I was selling fake crack in a different neighborhood and getting my money up to sell the real deal in my hood. I had my own little stash now. I'd hang out by the store with my money and wait for someone to buy me a Mad Dog 20/20. I'd drive my car from Skyway after hanging out and head to the CD (Central District.) After school I'd drive to different schools and pick fights with any of the dudes who looked like they were trying to be tough. I was starting to build a reputation for myself, my hand game was undeniable I fought with precision there was no winning if you were up against me, I loved a good fight. The challenge excited me. Getting into all kind of trouble, I had some beef and I needed to make a statement.

The first time I saw a gun I was in 8th grade, it was a 357. I had a run in with the Dog Pound out of Renton and they tried to jump me. I was in the hood talking about it and they found out and threatened to come back to the school. My friend was willing it to sell me a piece for $200 with the bullets already in it. I didn't have my hands on any money I had to think fast. How could I get some money together to get this gun? Grandma was a treasurer of the church and she always kept money in the house.

When no one was in her room, I went in there and stole money from the stash grandma was in charge of for the church. I hooked up with my friend and put that $200 in his hand. Once I got the gun I couldn't stop looking at it! It was so pretty! Silver chrome, loaded and ready to go! I took the gun to the school and was waiting on the dog pound to come. I was ready to light that parking lot up like the 4th of July. While I was excited to get my hands on that gun, I was in boiling water at home.

I was getting chewed out on a daily basis for stealing the church money from my grandma and I denied it every chance I got. My grandparents knew it had to me and that I was lying and had taken the money. My grandparents were on a mission, they came to the school to confront me. I hid the gun in my bag and kept it with me at all times. In my 3rd period class my name was called over the loudspeaker. I had no idea why I was being called to the office I didn't do anything that day or even that week. I told my best friend Charles Yancey to watch my bag and I went to the office. Once I was called down to the office I wasn't allowed to go back to the class and I was trying not to panic.

My stomach dropped knowing I left the gun in my bag. I was tuned out from the yelling and carrying on from my grandma. I could only think of my backpack the whole ride home. Did Charles get it? Are they going to find out? Dang I should have taken my bag with me! Once we got home grandma, grandpa and mommy all went to town, why did I take it? What was I thinking? Why would I touch the lord's money? What type of heathen was I turning into? I heard them in the distance but my mind was back at the school in the classroom where I left my bag.

Hearing the doorbell ring my stomach dropped. I already knew my so called best friend didn't grab my bag. I took a break from the questioning to answer the door and it was the police and my teacher was in the background with my bookbag in his hand. My friend left the bag and the teacher found the gun when he was trying to find out whose bag was left behind. I was easily targeted with my notebook in the bag. My grandmother wanted to know who was at the door and told me to invite them in. The officers announced that they were there for Christopher Boles. They wasted no time cuffing me in the hallway. It was breaking my heart to hear my grandmother crying. She knew at that point that the money I stole went to the gun discovered in my bag.

What was I thinking? Why did I go as far as to steal from grandma for a gun? This wasn't my first time in a police car but this felt very different, I knew they were going to keep me this time. I was silent as I got in the police car. I toughened up and fought my tears. Being arrested in front of my family was emotionally disturbing. I felt ashamed because they knew I stole the church's money in order to purchase the gun. The disappointment in their faces was unforgettable and it was etched in my mind reminding me that I was failing them.

I was driven to Mission Creek, a detention for boys ages 12-17. I was sentenced to 8 or 9 months. When they pulled into the Mission Creek the car entered through the basement there were different people being processed I saw a homie of mine and called out to him "8 up" and he answered "Straight up." As I looked around it wasn't anything like the movies but then again I didn't know what to expect. The air was dry in the room they placed me in, it smelled stale with overflowing garbage as I awaited processing. I could see at least a hundred other kids my age all separated by glass and wood partitions. I thought I was going to have to prove myself when a homie asked me where I was from. I let him know immediately BGD deuce 8 and he gave me a pass I knew I was good they were g's too. I think he may have been from Union I wasn't too sure.

Everything was on the county's time and they weren't in a hurry. I was transferred to a different room where I was interrogated. My brick wall was up I wasn't about to show any signs of weakness. I was uncomfortable with the strip search. It was definitely more sickening than any movie could accurately portray. I was given a beige jumper that seemed to fit just right which made me mad because I knew they were playing me. They shackled my feet and it made me wonder what I did that was so serious that I needed to be shackled like a slave.

With my upbringing I knew I didn't belong here, I

felt like a murderer or something, how long were they planning to make me stay? All those Sundays in church how did I get here? When I had to walk in the shackles it was a process because it was so many doors to walk through. The doors were so heavy that when it slammed it was so loud it sounded like thunder. Each door opened upon the officer's badges being presented. Walking past the cells I felt more comfortable because I knew the majority of everyone locked up was from the CD (Central District.) They were calling my name which made me smile, I was among the homies. The demeanor of the officers changed I think they thought they were going to have an advantage over me. But the recognition I received let them know I wasn't a rookie in the streets, I had a great level of respect.

I was placed in a 4 man cell, even though I wasn't home at least I was comfortable. Everyone in my cell knew the same people we were all either BGD's or Deuce 8. We told stories and reminisced about when Macmall came to Union got chased out of there. We used to all hang out at Richland, it was like a parking lot at night. You had to be from the CD (Central District) if you were out there. When they came to town for shows E 40, and C Bo, would come through and show love. Deuce 8 and Union both had record labels. They were always around, Yukmouth did a record with the homies. Mac-Dre would come through too. It was all love when they came through, they were family. Gang life and hip hop went hand in hand from way back.

I felt homesick when I heard I was about to be sent up to the institution. I was sad that my family didn't visit me for 3 or 4 weeks. I went back and forth to court. I was sentenced to 36 weeks which seemed like a mighty long time. The institution was a two hour drive from Seattle. I didn't know what to think on the bus ride up to the institution I heard so much advice about how I may have to get down because they were 8 to a room. But come to find out I was able to room with the homies because the officers knew better then to place a BGD with a blood or any other rival gang, they didn't want those problems unless they felt it necessary.

My days consisted of being in the hole for fighting the majority of the time I was there. It was all gang related and old beef from being on the streets I didn't even get to go to school or anything I was busy fighting rivals. The tank had a variety of gangs and that's where the majority of the fights took place. I always ended up setting it off when someone tried to dictate what show we were going to watch. When someone went to change the channel I knocked them right out, that was my way of claiming my territory .

One time I got so mad I knocked the TV right off the wall and I immediately was sent to the hole for 60 days. My tag line was "I'll beat you up boy!" I was always fighting behind one of the homies or how one looked at me seeming to try and size me up. The soon to be victim would try to cop out, knowing the outcome. "I ain't even got no beef with you Too Sick." I moved up in the ranks because I was down to defend my folks and I had a reputation of having hands as they would call it. I demanded respect and I always got it. If you didn't respect me there was going to be a problem and some consequences.

Being in the hole I was all by myself, I couldn't get no commissary, no phone calls I was allowed out of the room for one hour a day. In that time I was expected to shower, exercise and handle my phone calls all within 60 minutes. I spent the majority of my time writing letters to girls, some i didn't even know, and exercising and doing my push-ups. I didn't have any visitors because I was always in the box and it was at least a two hour drive. When my family did come the one or two times that they did come through, they let me know they were extremely disappointed in me, and what hurt the most is that i didn't blame them. We spoke on the phone at least once a week. I hated that I disappointed them, part of me felt like a loser but *only* because i knew i made choices that i had no business making, I knew better. But in essence I didn't care because to everyone else I was that dude.

3 CHAPTER THREE

I was in and out of the hole like a groundhog that couldn't make up its mind. I couldn't be controlled even in an institution. But when loneliness got the best of me I'd comply with the officers, listen to what they said, next thing you know I'm out in general population, yes, another form of manipulation. It wouldn't last too long because I'd find myself in another fight heading right back to the hole for the same thing, my temper. It took a few people to pull me off of somebody once I was on them. It's like I was in a zone, I blacked out once I made contact.

Fighting seemed to be how I expressed myself, earned respect, made my point, and controlled situations, it became apart of my life. I started boxing at 14, I was great according to the streets, but now I'd be learning the skills and technique of professional boxing. As I moved up the ranks of amateur boxing, I gained the attention of many people for being a **"Golden Glove Boxer."** My participation in with the bumble bees was an attempt to keep me out of jail.

I was great at fighting but now I was learning the skills and technique. I loved fighting, it was my thing but I still needed to learn self-control. In any fight if I got hit in the face I blacked out completely and i'd fight long after the bell rung. "Boles! You can't go off like that man!" my trainer yelled out nearly every fight. As I sat in the corner getting doused in water waiting on the next round I'd be reminded that getting hit in the face is not personal its part of the sport. I understood it as long as it wasn't actually happening. Once a boxer's glove made contact with my face I'd lose my mind fighting way past the bell all over again.

I didn't have the support of my family with boxing although it was an attempt to correct my behavior and find a positive outlet with my passion of fighting. The women in my family felt it was too violent but my trainer and my uncle were in my corner all the time. My uncle saw it as a great way for me to relieve all my pent up anger. He was always there rooting me on. Some of the homies would come out and support me sometimes. I boxed until I was 16 years old. I was still caught up in the street. When I reported before a fight I had to submit a urine analysis. In the beginning I was good but then after a while it kept coming back positive for marijuana.

I was released from the bumble bees and my trainer was disappointed that I couldn't stay sober in efforts to make something of myself. I didn't care though I was into the streets, hanging with my BGD family, smoking, drinking, chilling and making my presence felt when necessary. I said it didn't matter and I didn't really think it did but I didn't have any structure in my life at this point. Without the influence of my trainer and the schedule I had tried to adhere to I wound up back in jail.

My behavior was suicidal, my life was all about fighting, smoking and the gang life. My attitude was a shrug of the shoulders, and I was uncontrollable, I was furious inside. I was constantly disappointed in my father and he was only a town over. Why couldn't he come check on me? Why didn't he show up and try to make his presence known or felt more often? Hadn't he heard about me in the streets? Didn't he care?

I remember as a little boy waiting on him when he said he was coming. I picked out my own clothes and brushed my teeth and I sat on the sofa waiting for him out of excitement. I sat there until dinner time and nearly had to be pried from the sofa, I didn't want to go to sleep just in case he came and I missed him. When mom came to me with food I'd decline, "I'm waiting to eat with my dad, he said we're going to McDonalds. He never came and I would give my mom a tantrum for something she had nothing to do with.

My baby sister and I have the same father but she gravitated to my step father so she could care less whether our dad showed up or not. It didn't matter how many fights I had and won, how many ranks I moved up in the hood, I wanted my father. But he didn't know how to be a father nor did he take his responsibility seriously when it came to me I felt. It made me feel worthless when he didn't show up. Where did I belong? I felt like an outsider. My grandpa was there but I wanted my dad. Grandpa taught me how to ride a bike, drive a car, and play baseball. While I appreciated learning when we were out there the other kids were out there with their fathers not their grandfathers.

As I sought a sense of belonging, I sold drugs, drank, smoked, shot guns, fought and the more destructive I became the more love I got from my BGD family. I didn't get the same love at home. We weren't on the same page in my house, we didn't see eye to eye. I didn't see school as a place I needed to be. When out in the street there was an undeniable freedom no matter what time of day it was. My mom was at her wits end with me and my nonchalant attitude about school and my violent temperament. I was moving every few months and changing schools in efforts to be housed in the best environment. In reality mom was wasting her time,

I went from auntie to auntie, uncle to uncle, and I even went to my dad's for a little while. I wasn't into the school thing and wherever I went I was assessed and placed in a new school. It didn't matter what school I was placed in I had no interest.

My moving from town to town piqued my interest and brought more awareness to "Too Sick," the nickname given to me by BGD. It had taken over my life completely and I was above the law as far as following anyone's rules. One of the smoker's I was cool with got me an apartment in his name. I was selling dope out of the apartment and allowed my customers to buy the dope and get high in the apartment. It felt good to have my own space sometimes but it wasn't anything glamourous about my lifestyle or the apartment. It didn't resemble my boy "Scarface," but I was as reckless as he was and everyone knew not to cross me. I was set up in a dangerous part of Seattle, the police were always lurking which meant I was constantly watching my back.

Living on my own wasn't everything I thought it would be, I was eating fast food all the time, missing those home cooked meals from grandma. I was getting shot at and running for my life as I fired back at the enemy. Living in an apartment full of junkies and dope fiends it was hard to feel safe, I wasn't getting any sleep. Addicts have no loyalty, their main concern was getting high and getting the money to do so. They stole from each other, robbed people, and spent every dime they had just to get high. They were greedy when it came to the drugs and were recklessly chasing the high, I was entertained when they fought over the last couple of puffs. It didn't matter how much money I made or what I wore, I had to watch my back especially around these addicts first, and the streets second.

I had my own spot for about five to six months before I found myself in trouble once again. I got caught in Tacoma with a gun and was now facing time in the institution once again. I was in the bus station and spotted this lady counting money sitting by herself. Once she put the money in her purse I snatched the bag from her and got on the bus that was about to pull out of the station. As I sat on the bus I was hoping it would move anticipating to jump off at the next stop, but the woman whose purse I snatched had called the police. They boarded the bus, identified me and found my weapon on me took me to juvenile. I was charged with possession of stolen property and possession of a firearm. I was sentenced to eight months and was sent up to the institution.

When I got out, I went right back in! I was on the block celebrating my homecoming and someone decided that that day should be my last. They shot at me and I pulled my gun out and shot them down. Just before my 16th birthday I was sentenced to one year, my life was revolving around the streets and jail and breaking the cycle seemed to be light years away. I was released at 17 years old and headed straight to the CD (Central District) to see what was up. Caught up with Deuce 8, celebrated drinking, smoking, and just as I was getting used to being "outside," I'd get locked up.

I was embarrassed to contact my family and tell them what was going on with me. But they are my family and I would really realize that I missed them especially when I had no access to them. Hearing their voices on the phone would get me emotional which would mean a beat down for somebody later on. And of course that would lead me right to the hole. During those phone calls I'd promise to do better, I was convincing them and trying to convince myself that I was capable of living a normal life. But once freedom was right at my feet all the "promises," became a figment of my imagination. I didn't finish school, I wasn't interested in going to a prom so I didn't feel like I was missing anything. My future consisted of making money and Deuce 8.

My boy Kenny Smith and I were hanging out one night coming from downtown. Kenny got into a fight and whipped that kid something serious. We were almost home before a car drove up and took a left, it slowed up, we showed our Deuce 8 sign and kept walking. The car went down the block and came back around and started shooting! We ran but Kenny got shot! He got hit bad, blood seemed to be coming from everywhere and he died right in my arms. I went to the hospital with the body and was questioned about the guys and whether or not I knew them or not. I didn't know them, I had no idea of who killed my best friend.

The night kept replaying itself in my mind for months and I'd have nightmares. In the dream I could hear the gunshots ringing out and seeing Kenny struggle to breathe. I watched the blood leave his body and surround me as I held him and was helpless to bring him back to life. I was pissed off! Kenny was like my brother, we did a lot of things together and now he was just a memory. His death kind of humbled me as I found out how real death was. I was left with a case of the "what if's," what if we left earlier instead of trying to get more money, what if I shot homeboy when they first had the fight? What if it was me?

4 CHAPTER FOUR

Hebrews 11: Now faith is the substance of things hoped for, the evidence of things not seen

wound up moving to Tacoma with my aunt when people realized I was causing too much trouble. I was kicked out of the house. I went downtown Seattle, ran into Geno my 1st cousin.

"You doing too much, he said. Get away do something different." He encouraged me to go to Tacoma which prevented me from retaliating against the people that killed Kenny.

I went to stay with auntie Jab for a little while. I remember the day we went down there. We got off the bus and walked that night. We were hungry and about to stop in Burger King, Taco bell it was packed seemed to be a busy area. I had a lot on my mind as we stopped at KFC, we ran into this dude who referred to *himself* as a blood. Nothing popped off... same dude rolls around mean muggin' me, and they got out of the car. He started shooting immediately and we dropped low to the ground.

I started running but I when I looked back and saw that my cousin fell and I ran over and jumped down on the ground next to him making sure he was ok. When I saw he was ok, I ran into the Taco Bell looking for the shooter because he had on a Taco Bell uniform. We were upset and making a scene with customers and all. I smacked the condiments onto the floor and was not hearing anything the workers were saying to me. They threatened to call the cops, I dared them and I stood right there when they called. Dude was already in trouble for a different shooting his fingerprints were on the shells, and my cousin and I didn't cooperate with the cops.

I received a subpoena to testify against him but I didn't testify. Thomas, the shooter was arrested a month later following the shooting and is still in jail. My aunt was pissed off she wanted me to get myself together but it was my cousin who introduced me to the game. My aunt wasn't about to hide me, she reached out to my mom and let her know I was safe. My other aunt who lived in Lakewood was strict with me as far as going to school and I was compliant until I got kicked out of Lake High school for fighting. I was then referred to an alternative school, American Lake. My aunt muddied my name a little by using my information to turn on her phone and cable and didn't pay the bills.

Lakewood hustlers, used to hang out at Thunderbird apts. I heard they were supposed to jump me, I went to the store, had my gun on me. I had gathered a clique overtime and was introducing them to gang life. I took the clique with me and I stepped to Baby C Money and I wanted to address them and let them know I was ready. They were in the car, no one was ready to fight.

"I'm right here, you don't have to look for me, I'm right here in your hood." I stayed ready for war, ain't nobody had nothing on Too Sick!

Lakewood Hustlers rolled up to the school looking for me because the dudes I approached at the store *weren't* part of the gang. I pulled out my gun when the argument got heated. Someone called the cops, I didn't run but I threw the gun in the bushes. It had to be the kids I ran past that told on me. Somebody must have seen me toss the gun because it wasn't long before it was recovered. No one was hit, I told the cops I was shooting in the air to scare the people away from me. I had my alibi ready to go! I used the fact that I lost my friend in a shootout so I was afraid!

My alibi sort of worked for me, my sentence was light I got six months for possession of a firearm on school property. I was sent to Raymond Hall for Juveniles and then I got sent up state to a group home, more of a rehabilitative residence. I think it helped me to grow somewhat, had me thinking about my future which is something I wasn't really doing before. I had time to think, I wasn't fighting like I normally did and I kind of bonded with some of the counselors in there. I was changing my thought pattern and not going off the way I normally do. I became more observant before reacting.

Once I was released I stayed away from the gang a little bit because I didn't feel the love. The homies didn't look out as much as before. I got a little wisdom while I was in there, I went to school and actually paid attention. I didn't fight as
much which kept me out of the box. I was still selling dope and getting money though. I was maturing, my style of dressing changed too. I went from wearing dickies and chucks to slacks/jeans with a button up or a sweater. My hair was tapered as opposed to a hat cocked to the side. I was an OG. I was just into making my money. I think the counselors shed a little light on the way I living my life. Something in their words hit home for me. I took a long hard look at myself, who was I? Is this the way I really wanted to live my life?

I started dating which also put me in a different space. I met a girl named Yolanda in Green Tree which is a part of Skyway, my hood. I think the first thing that attracted me to her was that she had her own place. She was a rider and offered me her place to cook up the crack, she knew the ropes and made my life as a hustler a bit smoother. My girl had the hook up with blow up phones, I used to call my customers from a payphone. I was on a different level now, instead of going out shopping I started sending the smokers out to get her purses and clothes. Anytime they saw me at the spot they saw me with her.

With me having a stash spot I was able to get more drugs, and my wardrobe was upgraded. Yolanda was gangster and seasoned she taught me *not* to get money and eat in the same place, she had the idea of living in a more secluded area outside of Skyway, it was a high-rise in Tucwila. It was about 15-20 minutes from the CD (Central District) and 8 minutes from Skyway. We had the timing down to a science regarding how I was moving. I knew it would take more than 8 minutes for the police to catch up to me and they couldn't touch me if I was out of their jurisdiction. With a more intellectual mindset I didn't sell anything in Tuckwiller, I only sold outside the jurisdiction.

Yolanda and I were in and out of town to California to get dope, the quality was different. The fiends were loving it and it flew out of my hands every time I made a purchase. I couldn't keep a full stash, it was too popular. But with money comes problems and I found out through someone who tipped me that the feds were watching me. Yolanda was there when he told me this, she and I talked and decided I would no longer be the person making runs. There was this white smoker dude that would make runs for me and he would take the dope and distribute it to the customers for me. I was smartening up and thinking smarter, I had to get below the radar. In order to appear like a normal square couple, we even got part time jobs.

We were constantly trying to outsmart the system, I had no intention of going back to jail. Yolanda brought me to a whole different level of thinking and maturity. I even played step dad to her children, I was seriously way more mature than I'd ever been in my life. With my new found way of thinking which I owed to my rider, I decided to make it official. I copped her a ring that blew her mind and we got married on 1/15/99. Things were looking good for us and 4 days later she got a job which she started on 1/19/99. I also got a job and was supposed to start on 1/23/99.

I copped my case on 1/18/99 and I was hot because the group Yolanda gave $200 credit to were Crips. She was warned not to front them any drugs because they were known for playing games with the money. I wanted to go the night of 1/18/99 but didn't. I dropped Yolanda to work, I called Jack, the white fiend that distributed for me and we headed over to the trap house. I loaded my step kids into the car. I didn't intend on being there too long, I was there to get my bread.

I banged on the door one good time and announced myself, "It's C Crazy!" I kept banging on the door and they were fumbling. They were taking a while to answer and I was getting agitated. When they finally opened the door I had a heart to heart letting them know I was not there for the games. I was about my money. We started arguing because they were trying to get me to take their tv, radio, stereo, and VCR, not once did they say anything about money. The kids were restless and got out of the car to use the bathroom at the same time dude got slick with his words. I pulled the gun out and bashed him in the face with the barrel knocking him to the floor.

My uncontrollable temper had flared up which had been suppressed for so long, the rage immediately took over since they were testing me. I shot dude in the head with the kids standing right next to me, I never even heard them scream. I was on the hunt as I wanted no witnesses. Someone in fear of their lives jumped out the window, breaking the glass. There was glass flying through the air as I ran after the people in the house shooting at anything I thought had a pulse. When all appeared to be still, I bounced.

I jumped in the car, made sure the kids were straight and told my driver Jack to stop at the 7/11. With my temper still flaring I was about to shoot this dude I had a problem with in there but I saw a helicopter in the distance. I went home to Tuckwiller and changed my clothes and went to

McDonald's, Yolanda's new job and tried to convince her leave but she wouldn't budge she was a nervous wreck about the whereabouts of her kids. She could sense that something bad happened and demanded to know where her kids were.

"What did you do? Where are my kids" She asked frantically. "I'll tell you later, they outside in the car." I followed her out the door to the car.

When I stepped outside there were police cars everywhere, the officers had their guns drawn, cars were coming from every direction. There was nowhere to run, there were police cars from four different counties hunting for me. It looked like a scene from a movie when someone goes on a killing spree. My life was flashing before my eyes at this dramatic capture of little old me that was about to take place. In this distance I heard a blood curdling scream from Yolanda fearing for the lives of her children.

With over 100 guns drawn at me, I felt like my life was already over. I wasn't going to let them take me out. I took my gun out and put it to my head as my heart raced, I could hear it beating. As I searched the faces of the officers I could see them their mouths moving but couldn't hear them. All I knew was I was going to be in charge of what happened to me. My emotions were taking over because I couldn't believe what just took place. I never experienced this type of excitement before aside from when the police came to my school or the school bus to arrest me.

Yolanda started screaming "Don't do this!" She was crying hysterically, "please put the gun down!"

It was so much commotion at one time, "it doesn't have to end like this!" I could hear officers yelling. My hearing was extremely sensitive I heard everything so clearly I was overwhelmed. I heard cars on the road, people in McDonald's ordering, guns being cocked, Yolanda screaming and over all of it I still heard my heartbeat. I kept hearing Yolanda begging me to put the gun down and I dropped the gun watching it bounce a few feet away from me. I dropped to my knees and laid face down on the ground willingly.

I woke up in King County Jail in a red one piece high water jumpsuit with some socks and slippers on. I must have been in shock I don't remember being processed, or anything. I woke up in my tank. My thoughts overwhelmed me, wondering who told on me. Was I set up? Everything was going so good with me and Yolanda, I had a ride or die on my side. It must have been someone close to me to know my whereabouts like that. I had everything, a fully furnished apartment with brand new furniture. I had brand new cars freshly painted. I switched up my whole routine, I was moving real careful.... yet I had police from four different counties looking for me?

My name must have been on the map for a minute

with a close tail on my every move. It had to have been in order for me to get caught like that, was someone around me wearing a wire? I was determined to figure out who, what, where and why I was doing this bid. I was on the phone with anyone and everyone who may have had any information. I couldn't wrap my head around the fact that I was back here... behind the wall, again. I found out that there was a woman who was hiding under the bed. She must have been petrified and sung like a bird as soon as the police interviewed her.

I guess it must have been my time to get myself together completely. It's not like the homies didn't tell me that the feds were watching. I can't blame anyone for this but myself but there I was locked up 4 days after I got married. Thinking about it the marriage was more of a convenience, Yolanda was street smart and I learned a lot from her. But she was a rider for dudes in the game before meeting me, she knew the ropes. I trusted her but found out that she was easily persuaded and had her own agenda.

Yolanda wasted no time selling my dope, putting someone behind the wheels of my cars. Her behavior was reckless and I was shocked that she wouldn't honor her word. Til death due us part became until the prison door shut. She didn't take my calls, didn't write and it made me wonder if she played a part in having me set up.... having me watched. Had me wondering whether or not there was ever a debt of $200.00.

I know the love was real with the homies but during this bid I pulled away from the gangs and focused more on me. I could easily hear about what was happening on the street through anyone locked up with me that was BGD. I was into my case and found myself leaning on my grandmother for strength, I found myself yearning to talk to her and hear her wisdom. Worried about my case I often found myself asking for her prayers and guidance.

I told my grandmother the only plea I was getting was 42 years and I had to take it, as opposed to getting life. Grandma didn't believe that I would be sentenced 42 years and she encouraged me to pray. She said I don't see God giving you that. I wasn't in that space with her. I told her about my decision to plead guilty. I was getting nervous about a life sentence especially after being informed that one person I shot during the incident died. After speaking to my lawyer she said 15 years was on the table. Gramma was adamant about her gut feeling and told me don't sign anything, take it to trial. She said they don't know *my god like know my god.*

My attorney grew frustrated with me but I believed at the time that she had my best interest. After I informed her that I wanted to take it to trial, she quit. I was furious with my grandmother because now I had no one to defend me. I should have taken the 15 years but I had relied on gramma and her spiritual insight. I felt lost especially after I was appointed a court attorney, everyone knows that the court appointed attorneys don't work as hard. Gramma's gut instinct may cost me more than half of my life, my spirituality wasn't on the same plain as hers was and I was trying not to panic.

When I went back to my tank, all the homies ran up to me. They were anxious to hear about what happened in court. There I was discussing my case and hearing all kinds of things about the gun enhancements for the assault two and assault three. All this talk was making me nervous, while they were my homies breaking down the law... we were all in here for *breaking* the law. Funny how we should have been attorneys with all this knowledge, my jailhouse lawyers had me thinking hard about my case.

I found myself surrounded by Crips, homies to the people I shot during the incident. For six months of the bid it was on site for any Crip I saw that wanted it! Once again my hands were tested and they *knew* I had hands. It was the little dudes trying to make a name for themselves that wanted to test me. It wasn't anything new to me, I'd been locked up before, I fought before. This bid was bigger than any other because of the murder charge on my head. I wanted to be home, my son wasn't even 1 years old yet.

With my mind on the gun enhancements and the possibility of me never going home, I found myself thinking about my sisters. I missed them. I felt like i was never going to get out. That mind set got me into more trouble because I was thinking negatively, the hole became my new home once again. I was fighting every day, I was disrespectful to the correction officers. I felt like I was in this by myself, I had taken on a "me against the world attitude," and I dare anybody to come at me.

Jokes about me being crazy, which were lighthearted were taken negatively. The streets named me "C-Crazy," and "Too Sick," and they were surprised me when I reacted crazy and really got sick on them. No one was safe from me, I was at my wits end. I knew what I did and I knew I had to make it home but dealing with my reality was extremely painful. Even though I was in the worst position I was still a leader and the respect was there from the homies as well as the Crips.

My behavior was used to help my case, my lawyer was curious about why I was so violent. I easily answered because I don't care. That answer led me to having a psychiatric evaluation, according to the doctors my IQ was a 70! It was suggested that I had a mental health issue but they were still trying to prove that I could stand trial. At this time I was sent to Western state.

My documentation stated I was borderline retarded so I acted the part. I did things like talk to the phone with no one on the other line and was a total menace. I threw my medication across the room and refused to take it. I especially disrupted movie time.

I walked around with my t-shirt tied around my head and screamed throughout the hallways, I was fighting consistently, nothing soothed me. I tipped my food over constantly and refused to eat. I lost a considerable amount of weight due to my refusal to consume meals.

I was a nervous wreck during the onset of my trial, not knowing what to expect with it being my first trial with jurors judging me. I stopped fighting because I didn't want anything to affect my case. The medication I was on had me exhausted and I was not myself. I'd become lazy which was not me at all. With all my family present for the trial I was worried about what they would hear. They were about to find out who I was and the things I involved myself in so many years of terrorizing the streets. I found myself numb as I awaited my fate.

The whole experience played on my psyche. It had me thinking the prosecutor played games with me by staring at me and whispering to his team. I found myself sweating profusely in my slacks, shirt, tie and shoes. An outfit that made me look innocent, something I should have been wearing in church. Sitting in on this trial as they retold the story and examined it. I relived every moment which really made me sick to my stomach. The intensity of the courtroom was overwhelming, I was wishing it was a dream or an ill prank but as time went on reality set in.

I had to buckle up and face what God had in store

for me. I realized that there was a purpose in all of my madness but as I sat in court awaiting judgement I was clueless. Funny how as much as I've been in the streets and avoiding my family, they were the ones who were consistent in supporting me. I was raised better than this, how did I allow $200 measly dollars and street principles to dictate my future. I sat there questioning God, how could I allow myself to be involved in such nonsense. Why me? I don't deserve this! I sat in court and asked God to allow me to be a better person, to give me a chance to make him proud.

As quickly as I said the prayer, negativity set in. Why did I cooperate? How did I get caught? Next time I'll go by myself, it must have been the kids that slowed me up. As I sat there twiddling my thumbs I wondered what I would be doing outside right now. It's over for me man! There's no getting past this for me. I knew I was in trouble what would 12 jurors think of me and my crime? They were probably about to throw the book at me. What if I had gone the night before? I only refrained from going because Yolanda insisted that I go the next day. Scratch that it would have been more people there and that couldn't have been a better choice

I lost it all, the cars, the women, the money and I hated that I was locked up. As I listened to the evidence none of it sounded like me. It sound like "C Crazy," see for one year I hadn't touched any alcohol or drugs. Sitting there sober I listened to everything I did under the influence of laced weed.

My demeanor was different. from who they described me to be. I was ready to move on from whoever they were talking about, I wanted to evolve.

5 CHAPTER FIVE

For those of you who will hopefully never be placed in this predicament, there are two judges I had to sit before. The judge who heard all of the evidence and the judge who would sentence you. During this terrorizing week, I entertained myself by looking at the grid, this gave me an idea of how many years I would serve as the points added up. According to the grid I was looking at a sentence of 10 years a total of 120 months. Thinking of doing ten years had me sick to my stomach. As much as I wanted to change on one hand I went completely ballistic on the other. I was fighting anyone who looked at me funny. I disrespected the guard and was placed in the hole. I wasn't myself I was fearful and angry about my choices, how could I get out of this!

I had the hardest time resting because I was so

nervous, I tossed and turned, looked at the ceiling all night. I looked across from me at an empty tank. I could tell it was morning as the daylight crept into my cell and I could hear more than one set of footsteps. There were cells opening and closing, keys jangling against the officers as they made their way down the hall. As they approached my cell they yelled out "open up F 13." The door popped open and my soul dropped to my feet. I was instructed to turn around and was restricted by the three guards as cuffs were placed on my wrists and the shackles were placed around my waist, my wrists were joined to the shackles on my waist. There was limited movement as to how I could move my hands. An officer bent down to put the shackles on my feet, I was then led out with one guard leading the way and the other two on either side of me.

Heading over to the courthouse handcuffed and shackled from the waist down. I was in orange jumpsuit which defined that I was placed in the hole at *high risk.* Being high risk meant that I was a threat to the population as well as in the hole with the guards. I was in an IMU program which meant I had to be separated from the main population until I was sentenced due to my violent behavior. I had to walk by myself facing judgment that day and walked clumsily over the bridge to the court. Once I arrived I was informed that I was first on the docket.

I was surrounded by the three guards and the bailiff during the sentencing. The bailiff kept his hand on his gun as he anticipated an outburst from me. I was labeled as an animal one who committed a *careless act*. I sat there listening as the judge read all of the charges I was facing. He read the minimal and maximum possibilities. The judge surprised me with the statements he shared in the courtroom. He said I was a good guy who made bad decisions and who had future potential. His speech was uplifting which I didn't expect, and I got sentenced 36 months for the gun enhancement for the assault 2 and 18 months for the gun enhancement for the assault 3, and 12 months with the assault two. My sentences ran concurrent for the assault two and three which lessened my time.

I had to serve my gun enhancement off top there was no getting around that, which is why I was sentenced 48 months altogether. I was really expecting to do more time and while I should have been grateful because I could have gotten sentenced 10 years if it ran bowlegged.... but I only got 66 months. I was still down and out that I had to serve at all. When I got to my tank I sat down with my paperwork and tried to figure out how much time I had to do.

In the tank there are a mix of criminals that aren't the best or friendliest to mingle with and everyone is dealing with their own battles regarding sentencing. It was a very tense atmosphere. Lots of stare downs and gruesome fights as the men were enraged with themselves and the hand they were being dealt because of the way they led their lives.

In the midst of this is me trying to figure out how much time I'd have to serve. I was gearing my mind up to walk this out and do my time. I knew I'd be far from my family and the chances I'd see them often was far and in between.

I thought about the court appointed attorney that I had zero faith in, she was the one to get that home run! She was the one that got me the 66 months. And Grandma had been faith filled the whole time, I had a lot of learning to do and growing spiritually and mentally. Grandma was off by a few months but she surely said 5 years, 5 ½ ain't so bad. But right now I was relieved that it was 5 years instead of 10. I wish I didn't have to do anytime at all, I'll be 24 when i get out of here. I tried to see the positive but I was stuck with a negative mindset.

The following week I was waiting for my name to be called to get on the chain bus. I was on the Tuesday docket. I heard my name being called by C.O. "Boles, roll it up! You heading out!" I grabbed my things, a thin green mattress, brow itchy blanket, and some dingy sheets. I put my things in the middle of the mattress along with paperwork, pictures, letters, cosmetics and anything else that meant anything to me. When I got downstairs I was asked to separate the blanket, sheets and leave the mattress right there on the floor. I kept my personal things with me until I got downstairs.

When I got downstairs I heard so many voices from the BGD and a lot of people I was cool with, yelling out to me to keep my head up. They were telling me to be safe, they loved me, they'll be in touch, wanting to know how much time I got. I yelled back I got 6 years. they wanted to know where I was being sent. I answered back I don't know yet. If felt good to get the love from the homies. You're not supposed to talk in the tanks but I guess the C.O.'s understood and allowed it. some were even cool enough to allow me to walk up to a tank to give some love, I was even allowed to share food from commissary I couldn't take with me. I was honored that they allowed me to do this especially since I caused so much trouble. The C.O.'s probably knew I wouldn't do anything to further extend my time.

I went to processing where I was being prepared to be sent up to the penetentury. I was told to "spread em," as they searched me for any items I may have tried to smuggle out with me. I felt violated as I had to do this in a tank where 30 other people were in the room. I heard someone yell out, "man you better get used to it! You gon be taking a shower with like 50 dudes." They checked my personal belongings and issued me new clothing, another red jumpsuit, underwear, t-shirt, socks and brown slippers. I then went to the tank to wait for everyone being shipped out to finish changing their clothes and being searched. Once everyone was done we were told to kneel on a hard brown bench as the guards came through to shackle our feet and hands. For two hours we sat in the wating tank chained up waiting for everyone else to be processed, searched and chained.

Reality reared its ugly head as we were lined up to go outside and were led out to the bus. I felt relieved to be leaving the county jail, once in my seat I exhaled my head dropped and I was thankful to be leaving the county but anxious about the penententury. I thought about my mom's biscuits, my grandpa's banana pudding. I thought of my family and the reunions. I knew I'd be an adult when I got out, from 19 to 24 years old. I'd be missing so much! I thought of Yolanda and how she was acting up. I'd only been in for 10 months and she was already rumored to have been with the homies. I knew from hearing this that I may have been facing this bid by myself. She only came twice while I was in King County, she always had an excuse of why she couldn't visit as much. When I called her, she's avoid the call, or say she didn't hear it. There was always a lame excuse as to why we didn't talk as often. I guess it was out of sight out of mind for her.

I felt lonely … avoided by her and lots of people I attempted to reach out to and was unsuccessful. I felt abandoned, forgotten and frustrated whenever I hung up the phone when no one was available. After a short time I reminded myself that not everyone was on my time, and I needed to chill. I conquered my feelings of abandonment and I'd write letters or stand on the bench and look out the window. Resting my arms on the window on the ledge I'd start free styling making beats on the window sill until someone would join me. We'd end up at the round table freestyling and banging on the table until we were reminded where we were and that we were too loud and to break it up in the corner, Some of us scattered, some stayed and some went to the phones.

It seemed like every tank I was in, the guards were on me. As we neared the penetentury the miles flew behind me, I wondered what they categorized me as.... are they going to treat me differently? I'd heard the guards are way more aggressive, they can put their hands on you and get away with it. There was more to lose in the penetentury... I could lose good time which meant I could end up serving a full sentence.

Looking around the bus we were all in our own thoughts, some guys slept on the way to the Shelton, (Washington Correctional Facility.) Someone started a conversation with me which led to us talking about our cases and people we knew. I heard about homies that were killed, doing time or doing well. I was getting the scoop on the street, people in jail always knew what was going on outside. We had our own major news network on the inside. I saw some people I haven't seen in awhile and these dudes I knew would be doing this bid with me, at least I knew some people.

The bus turned off the freeway, and it took a back road with arrows and signs which indicated we were heading to Washington Correctional Facility. As we neared the facility I saw the towers, the barbed wire fences. I could feel butterflies in my stomach as I was about to enter unfamiliar territory. We pulled up to the facility as the officers called for support to remove us from the bus. The correction officers got on the bus and gave us our instructions, we were taken off in groups of two and led down the steps as our feet were shackled. We called it a "gangsta scoot," as our footsteps were very limited.

In processing we were searched, received our bedding and put in a holding tank. One by one we were called to the desk, but I chose to go first. I was fingerprinted and led to my cell. Passing the cells I was either greeted with a what's up, where you from? what tank you in? Lets meet up at chow, 8 up, straight up! I didn't know the dude they had me in the room with, he was a little goofy. He was laid back but I wasn't feeling goof troop. When I went to chow, I saw my homie.

"Yo Too Sick, who you in the cell with?" He asked, eyebrows raised.

"Some goofy dude. Where he from? I don't know from where, from nowhere," I answered shaking my head.

"Try to get in my room, I'm by myself." He offered as he went down the chow line.

I did try to get in his room but wasn't successful. I had to ride it out with Goofy. I was in Shelton for one week and sent to classification where I found out that in two weeks I would be going to Wala

Wala building in medium custody. When the homies heard that I was going to Wala Wala they told me all the war stories. It was the worst penetentury of the state of Washington. From what I knew all the homies were there so I wasn't too nervous. I was on guard because the people I had the case over were Crips, and their homies were in there too. I wouldn't allow myself to think about it too much. I'd deal with it when I got there.

The two weeks in Shelton flew by and before I knew it I was rolling up and heading to Wala Wala, I had to go through the search process all over again, roll up the mattress with the blanket, and sheets, and then separate them. I put on the jumpsuit, underwear, t-shirt, socks, and brown slippers. I was handcuffed, feet chained, and told to sit and wait for everyone else. The bus the ride was about 5 hours, and I fell out after looking at what seemed to be the same scenery. I was dropped off at medium security at Wala Wala.

The guards that rolled up to the bus were super hard in the face and they weren't friendly, they were aggressive and ready to get down if needed. We were all brought off the bus row by row but at the same time. We were told to face the bus, patted down and pulled by the shackled on our waists. I immediately had something to say "why you gotta be so rough I'm not a toy!" we undressed in front of the guards as they watched us undress. There was about 10 of us, and we each had a guard getting clothing for us. I was excited to be getting a pair of jeans. They weren't name brand but denim felt better than the jumper.

Me being me, I tried to sag my jeans which immediately caught the attention of the guards and I received a size smaller. In two weeks I was back in a jumper because I tried to sag and got noticed. I was placed in the cell with a homie as they avoided putting a blood, crip or BGD in the same cell as that would be a war. My homie gave me a run down of the jail and how things worked there. Who was there, when chow time was, where to walk, where I should be in the yard All the gangs sat separately and I was told where BGD sat to avoid conflict.

At chow I was shown the homies of the people affiliated with my case. My homie knew me well and he wanted me to know who was who. Everyone had an idea of who I was and they knew my case. Once my name started ringing bells by phone call or wire via the jail, it was about to be on. After chow I was with the homies as we got up, the Crips got up and they left out with us. We were all lingering and they said what's up and I said what's up? I already know who they were, I was cocky and ready to fight, we sized each other up. It got tense but the guards in the tower saw us and said "keep it moving." my homie kept me from getting shot by the guard in the tower. We went to the day room and chilled out there, talked and got caught up.

A few days later I was on the phone outside and this dude ran up on me. This dude about 6 feet, brown skin, looked like a gym rat, he had two scraggly long braids hanging down, look like they been in there for a while. Dude was like

"Ain't ya name too sick?" He squinted.

"Yeah the one and only!" I answered, standing tall.

"You killed my homie!" He growled and leaned closer to me.

"Which one? I stared at him, ready to knock him out.

"Oh you a killer like that huh?" He asked cocking his head to the side, his arms folded on his chest.

"You said the name…... right." I said sizing him up.

Once i got off the phone I felt like it was about to was about to go down. Dude rushed out at me from the crowd while I was leaving the yard and I gave him a 3 piece. My hitting him sent the jail into a frenzy! They became loud and rowdy, they were anxious to see more but homie was in a daze. The commotion got the attention of the guards who came running over to where we were to break up the crowd in the breezeway.

I was still amped up and my homies were pushing

me away from the incident. It looked like ten or more guards were coming straight to me, they handcuffed me and took me straight to the hole. I was trying to tell them that I defended myself from the dude rushing me. Somebody ratted me out and they sent me to the hole for 20 days. After the 20 days I met with a counselor where I found out that I was being sent to 6 wing maximum security.

When I got back from classification to the hole, the person in the next cell asked me what happened. I told him I was heading to Six Wing and he told me that that was a rowdy wing and it was full of young lifers who fought all the time. I felt like I was being set up to fail. I was trying to chill and just do my time. But I was ready for whatever so I looked forward to the new scenery. Homie in the hole with me created a fishing line where he'd tie snacks to a string and he'd shoot it out like a yoyo and it was tied to a comb for the weight. We'd exchange candy, sweets, things we didn't eat from chow and sort of built of a brotherhood from that.

Those 20 days flew by and my brotherhood with the homie I never met ended quickly. The day I left the hole, two C.O's came and got me, I was going to the main population. Finally no handcuffs or shackles, I went straight into a cell which happened to be occupied with some people that I knew on the F tier. There were four people per cell and this was so different, I've gone from sharing a cell with two people, to being in the hole to now being in a cell with four people. There was no privacy what so ever, the toilet was right there on the left in front of everyone.

I didn't think of the claustrophobic atmosphere too much because I was among my homies that I haven't seen for years. This was different there were no doors, there were bars. It really hit me that this is where I'd be spending my time for the next 5 years. I kind of felt comfortable because when I went to the chow hall I knew almost everyone. All my homies that I stopped seeing in the hood were in here doing time.

The og's and the little homies were in there, back from OSC "Out school crushers," or "Out seeking crime," all BGD affiliates. Closed custody location didn't matter anymore because everyone I knew was there. I felt protected with my homies there, I knew they wouldn't allow anything to happen to me. The Crips knew I was there but no one tested me because my homies were so deep and everyone knew about what happened in Medium Security.

A Blood I was cool with, shared a cell with me and was really going through it. He was so consumed with being ignored by his children's mother. She didn't take his calls or visit him. He was always talking about it. We teased him about being soft as a way of trying to cheer him up or to leave the situation alone but he would get violent if people joked with him pertaining to his girlfriend. One day coming back from Chow and we came back to the cell to find Bowlegged Lou hanging by an extension cord. We were bugging out that he did that, and we were all placed in the hole as they investigated his death. Our cell became a crime scene and letters were found of his heartbreak and suicidal intentions. Once the investigation was clear we were able to return to our cell.

The death of Bowlegged Lou had a different effect on me..... Bowlegged Lou weakened before my eyes, this wasn't his first rodeo. I can't believe he took his life! I was really shocked that he did that. I can't imagine my emotions over a woman making me end my life. The devil really had a hold of him when he tied the rope, stood on the toilet, and tied the extension cord around the tv stand and jumped off.

That day replayed repeatedly in my mind so vividly while I was in the hole. Before we went to Chow we were laughing and smoking weed in the cell. With our smoking cypher we were switching posts with one of us smoking at the bars to throw the guard off. When we came back from Chow to the cell we saw Lou hanging. There he was in the back of the cell hanging and we immediately put our flag out to get the attention of the guard. We were calling out to Lou with no response from him and we were yelling for the guards to come.

The guards came over the intercom and asked what we wanted, we told him the homie was dead. There was an announcement made and the hallway was filled with correction officers. We were all placed in handcuffs and taken to the hole. We were informed that it was normal procedure for us to be taken to the hole in a situation like this. I was hoping that the weed wasn't laced and that it wasn't our fault.

The death of my cell mate took me back to my childhood, I got creative. I stacked three trunks to use as podium and made a microphone out toilet tissue rolls and made the shampoo bottle my mic stand. I used my popularity in a different way to spread a message. I was familiar with the bible and used it to share messages in my sermons. It became my thing to do before chow performing and having church right in my cell. My sermons were the talk of the chow time which made me feel good.

I remember one time in the chow hall I announced that I was done with the gang life. Something came over me and I felt the need to make the announcement to my homies and they thought I was buggin out. I got irritated and we went back and forth about my decision. I got up from the table and left and was immediately followed by two people sent in to jump me. The end result for the followers was reconstructive surgery and the other was knocked out cold.

I was the wrong one to be on the receiving end of being jumped. It was some BGD's that I knew but I wasn't really close with that tried to set me up. An OG was sent my way and I got the best of him. He turned it around wanting to be my friend all of a sudden I was his homie. He was trying to claim he didn't want to do me like that, he tried to act like he gave me the upper hand. He was in there trying to negotiate and chose to try to befriend me. I knew that something like that may happen but thought my seniority gave me respect so I was genuinely surprised to see that happen. I didn't think they would jump me, that blew my mind.

My creativity didn't end with the makeshift church in my cell, I was also a chef. We made summer sausages on the back of the toilet by putting them on a pencil and roasting it. Depending on how fast you wanted to cook, you either wrapped tissue loosely or tightly around your hand and placed the tissue on the back of the toilet. The very top of the makeshift tissue grill was lit and placed on the back of the toilet and we'd start our barbecues. From our menu we had ramen noodles with the summer sausage, burrito, and a spread of nachos, and sometimes we'd recreate our dinner from chow on the makeshift grill.

Although I decided to leave the gang life alone I was still active due to my seniority. I was still wreaking havoc and the CUS (Correction Unit Supervisor) had grown tired of me. He brought me in and gave me an ultimatum of good behavior for six months and I'd had a choice of where I'd want to go. He felt as if I was a threat to the penitentiary and he'd had enough. I'd had enough of being there and was truly a bully. If you bumped into me I'd slap you in the face. I'd run up in cells if that's what

I felt like doing. But having this opportunity to leave and start anew was attractive to me so for 6 months I behaved.

I chose to spend the rest of my time in Aberdeen this was a new jail where they were looking for people to come in. I was able to get visits and immediately found a girl to bring me weed to sell. The way I broke the weed down it brought me in $400 for a $20 sack. My girl, Melanie came up once a week for about 8 months until someone told on me. Her car was checked and but they only found a blunt in the glove compartment. I never had a chance to approach the dude who set me up because they got me up out of Aberdeen and shipped me right back to Wala Wala this time in the 8 wing. Once again I was with the homies and that's where I rode out the rest of my time.

6 CHAPTER SIX

On a rainy and cold Sunday afternoon in February 2004 I walked out of Wala Wala Maximum security feeling real fresh with fresh white t-shirt, crisp jeans and some chucks. I made sure my jeans were starched with sugar and water. I made sure to steal a spray bottle and made the solution. I sprayed my jeans front and back and placed them under the mattress for two days. After sleeping on those jeans for two nights they were able to stand up on their own. I walked out of there with only my release papers and the determination to be successful.

At the gate waiting for me was my girlfriend Melanie who had a ride from my homie's wife. I told them to take me straight to Bethany Temple Pentecostal church in the CD (Central District.) As soon as I walked into the church I felt refreshed. I was there to surprise my family, they knew my release date but I kept the time to myself. My parents and grandparents were so happy to see me we all broke down crying. It had to be the most emotional service, I'd been to in years.

Bethany Temple was turned up with happiness and the sermon was filled with a powerful message which seemed personalized. I felt all the love that I'd been missing, the spiritual music filled me up in a way I can't put in words but it was amazing. Even while incarcerated I'd stopped listening to rap music and chose gospel to start and end my days. I needed the encouragement in my darkest hours.

After church I asked Melanie to drive me through the hood we hit Yessler and said what's up to a few homies. I had to let them know I was good, let them see me fresh out. They offered me some smoke which I declined because I was on parole but I did take a cup of Hennessy to the head. In keeping my word to my family I was heading back to my grandmother's house. I made a quick stop to Melanie's where she had been holding my mint condition red BMW, black interior with the sunroof. I saved the money I made from the weed I sold in Aberdeen and had her buy the car and save it for me. With all that we made together even she was able to get a brand new car. Although I didn't have my license, I was feeling real lucky and chose to drive on my own.

When I knocked on grandma's door, they yelled

"surprise," I was shocked. My son Deondre came running up to me, I grabbed him and loved him up. I introduced Melanie to my family as my girlfriend and we were soon seated at dinner. My mom introduced me to Patricia, the legal guardian of my son and we got into a deep conversation about Deondre and how she got custody of my son. With the dinner party being so loud we wound up off to the side as she caught me up about my son's mother and how she abandoned my son. This conversation didn't sit well with Melanie who felt left out, she was so upset with me that she left my grandmother's house without saying good night.

I called Melanie to find out what was going on and she became irate saying I disrespected her by entertaining someone right in front of her face. The thing is Melanie felt guilty for neglecting me for six months, not accepting my calls or writing me. She was in a relationship with a woman which I found entertaining but she didn't think it was so funny. Her guilt had her thinking I was being disrespectful when in reality I was really just being informed about my son. I let her know that I was freshout with no intention of arguing with her, since she was gone for six months before and I didn't miss her she could be gone now and I wouldn't miss her! I wasn't about to make myself upset after such a beautiful night filled with the love and the home cooked food from the dinner party.

My cousins wanted to keep the party going and go to the Muckleshoot Casino in Auburn for some drinks and catching up. I invited Patricia to come and hang out with us since we were getting along so easily. I shared my war stories over drinks and had their mouths hanging open. My family embraced me regardless of the time lost and the way I led my life. They wanted better for me and I wanted the same thing. They had me promise to try harder to live better. They didn't know what was going on because I held all of my pain in, as well as what actually went down the day of my arrest. We broke night which is something I hadn't done in years. I enjoyed myself and I truly appreciated my freedom.

Patricia and I maintained a cool relationship and I spent a lot of time around her. She found it odd that for someone coming out of prison I was so respectful with her. She even surprised me with questioning my sexuality which was truly a challenge and a joke. Our rapport brought us closer to where we had a relationship and I became a live-in. On November 5, 2005 we welcomed my daughter Deslaree Gabriel into the world. She was my booga, my princess, my lil baby! Everytime I looked at her I had another nickname for her.

Patricia and I didn't make it because she wanted the person that I used to be. The person I was trying desperately to get away from, "Too Sick." I had grown smarter and learned how to get around a few things, I was in car wreck and that became my new hustle. I'd get settlements from the insured cars and flip the money in the hood. I'd take $15,000 and buy half a bird, flip it and start all over again. Car wrecking became lucrative but every hustle don't last as long as we'd like. I invested in my apartment got new furniture, flat screen tv and drove a nice KIA put it on rims. I stayed fresh and life seemed good. I made sure they knew I was out here, I made a lot of noise. I stayed moving in and out of state, fast money, fast paced but I was able to manage.

Moving fast and making noise brought me unwanted attention eventually, I started getting pulled over by the cops. I slowed up and moved back to grandma's house after the police came directly to my door. I had just come from making a drop after 5 days away from my apartment, the unexpected knock threw me off. I was clean with no product. I answered the door to them saying there was a call regarding disturbance, when I said I hadn't been there they began questioning my whereabouts. All this sudden police presence had me nervous and I got out of the lease. I moved in with my grandparents and parked my Kia in the yard but then moved it into the garage.

I bought a bucket (Chevy Lumina) and chose to move a little slower. One day while washing my car I met a girl named Helena. If I hadn't slowed up I'd have never known she lived next door to grandma. Helena spoke to me and I was up for the challenge. My game was still up to par and we exchanged numbers. We became tight pretty fast and were soon inseparable. Helena was a rider, she was bold enough to take risks that would get me locked up. She also made sure I had 3pc with french fries and peach cobbler because she worked at a chicken spot.

Within six months I moved out of my grandma's place. After making money and being out all night I was loaded. Helena called me and started an argument with me because I didn't hear her phone calls. She kept demanding that I pick her up even though I was in no position to drive. I felt compelled to get her because it was so late but against my better judgement I went to pick her up. Here I was being accused of having a woman over, and having an affair, when all I was doing honestly was about to go to sleep before being forced to pick her up. I had enough of fighting with her, I stopped the car on Rainier Avenue and asked her to get out. She was mad that she couldn't come to my house. She swung on me and we tussled a little bit until she calmed down. I let her get back in the car and I took her home.

Helena was a wild one, she was still enraged and when she got out of the car in front of her house, she grabbed a bottle and threw it at my head. I got out to close the door on her side and she grabbed a stick to hit me swung at me and "Too Sick," came out. Next thing you know she was laying there on the ground bleeding I thought she was dead. I got out of there as I saw my life flashing before me. I went back to my apartment packed a bag and went to Portland, about 3 hours outside of Seattle.

I got multiple messages from the police saying they

needed to talk to me. Helena filled up my voicemail with threats of my going back to jail after hitting her with the stick. I came back to face the music and wound up getting arrested, I bailed out with $5,000. I had money on me so I had my cousin come get money off my books and bail me out. If only I listened when my conscience told me not to go get her.

In order to stay out of jail I made good with Patricia and made up with her. I convinced her to writer a letter to her attorney that she wanted to drop the charges. During this hood honeymoon phase my son, Terrell was born. Having a newborn in such a tension filled environment was difficult because of the violent nature of our relationship. The state picked up the case and I was in and out of court for a year. The weapon charge was reduced to an assault 4 charge. I was on probation for three years after defending myself from *her*. I wasn't even trying to be bothered with her that day! I chose to distance myself from Helena because I didn't trust her after that.

I met someone new and anytime Helena saw me with the new young lady together she called the cops claiming I assaulted her. She harassed me at my grandmother's house whenever she knew they went out of town. She tried to run me off the road a few times. Helena even had a no contact order against her from the young lady I was dealing with. Helena was forcing me to deal with her because it seemed to be the only way to keep her calm. She was controlling my life with 911. One day I was at my grandmother's house and she was banging on the garage door, as soon as I opened the door she attacked me!

Helena bit me! My sister and the young lady I was dealing with both came running out trying to break up the fight. Helena had a pit bull type of locked jaw biting deeper into my arm and wouldn't let go. I had hit her in the head to get her off of me. I wound up getting a tetanus shot from her biting me (and I still have the mark) and then I was on the run because she called the cops on me again!

I got tired of running after three months and turned myself in, I thought telling on myself would be a better outcome. But I still got locked up for 8 months. I was done messing with her, Helena had put me through more than I could stand. But she was faithful and she wrote me and put money on my books. Her good hearted nature of sending me money sent me to the hole. After quickly learning that lesson she wrote me under another name, and continued to send money. After that short bid I wanted nothing to do with her and tried to start my life anew. She spotted me out and about with someone new and called the police and started again with her lies. Helena knew that calling the cops and saying my name with so many arrests and bids that I was guaranteed to get locked up.

A few days later, I was pulled over for the tv's in

my car. The tv's were in the back of the headrest as well as the dashboard, but they weren't playing a movie it was only reading the track which was playing. With me being pulled over he ran my name and I was locked up on the spot! Not for the tv's, for violating the no contact order, and a violation of my probation. As I sat in there for three months, I wound up writing Helena and trying to patch things up with her. Once I got out and decided to make things right with her. For a few weeks we got along really well before our relationship became rocky again. I couldn't make it right and decided that once again I'd leave her alone.

With us being on the off again period Helena tried to run me off the road again! she saw a young lady in my car and tried to kill us both! With such a near death experience I went to the police trying to complain on her and found out I have five violations of no contact I wasn't aware of. To top it off I had $10,000 of unsold crack cocaine in the car so upon the search I was handcuffed and arrested.

The judge was tired of me. He let me have it in the courtroom told me off about going back and forth to jail over this scorned woman. He offered me an option, I left Helena alone and he'd revoke my probation after 13 months in jail. I was sent to RJC where I was fighting too much and was transferred to Yakima jail. In Yakima it was heavily populated with Mexicans, there were plenty more fights due to the language and cultural barrier. I fought nearly every day, and I got stabbed while I was in my tank.

When I got released from Yakima Jail my life really took a shift for the better, that jail woke me up. I fought everyday and I was exhausted. I didn't want to have to live like this anymore, something had to give.

7 CHAPTER SEVEN

Proverbs 14 *Every wise woman buildeth her house: but the foolish plucketh it down with her hands.*

I continued to pay for my life choices as there was nowhere for me to be paroled. With having so many priors and my life of crime within the south end, Central District and Skyway. My name rang so many bells in a negative light that I wasn't wanted in any of these areas as a resident. This kept me from my current significant other as well as my family and the homies. I would really be starting off on a fresh foot. My release date was held back for two weeks because I couldn't find an address to be released to.

My mind went back to the question of "if you could

ask God of one thing and you know that he would change it what would that be?" I wanted love, I wanted to be free. I hated that I was still locked up because I couldn't go anywhere. My attitude became intolerable, I was nasty with the officers, at this point I was feeling like a caged animal. I was sent to the hole during this time, where I seemed to have spent a lot of time during my bids. It literally brought me to my knees because I'd have enough. I was weakened to praying for my sanity, my patience, I was being purged of my habits during these tiresome two weeks, I had no other alternative but to trust God.

Only he truly knew my heart, I had so many plans once I got out of here! I was ready to go! What was the hold up? How could I be banned from living in the places I grew up? I was ready for change I could feel it within me. My prayers were becoming stronger while I was in the hole. I wrote 7 sermons for a 7 day revival during this time but I wasn't even a pastor. Yes this gang member, this convict, God spoke to me during this process. Everything that was being said to me I didn't fully understand but I knew that God was in control and was using these two weeks to mold me, develop and rebuild my heart during this process. It was necessary to be isolated during this rebuilding. There would be no distractions as there was no one beside me on either side of me. I was in the unit completely by myself. God was working with me and I was forced to be obedient.

During this time God told me to call my dad who lived in Auburn, near the south end. It was a nice neighborhood and my dad was in agreement to use his address. I was so happy to be released! I remember going to the store to get a Mickey and a black and mild to sit back and chill with. My body immediately rejected the beer and I unwrapped the black and mild and smoked a little of the black and wild I got nauseated with a headrush. I put it out. My body was completely clean and wanted none of the toxins I was accustomed to emptying into it for so many years.

The young lady that did the bid with me came and got me the next day as I was in celebratory mood. However, a few miles down the road I asked her to stop the car and for her to take me back to my dads house. She was upset with me and refused to take me back and she kicked me out of her car. I respected her wishes and I walked back to my father's house. He was surprised to see me back so soon, but I let him know it was best for me to be home.

I started spending more time with my grandmother, I became a consistent visitor at the church. My desire to know more led me to attending more services during the week. I was now attending bible study during the week and took the big leap to be saved after a month of attending church. I was saved on a Sunday. I was tired of being sick and tired and I was determined to do something different. While the preacher was preaching I thought of everything I tried; the streets, selling drugs, making money, women, and numerous jail bids. All of this and I haven't tried God. I was in church having a war within my head, how can I replace the money? Show me how I can replace the money, show me how I can live life. All I know is the gang life how I can survive in these streets? The war in my mind pushed me up and out of my seat and it wasn't even time for the alter call. God showed up and showed me who was in control. He showed me right then that he would lead me in the right direction. I went right up to the altar and asked God to save me from me, save me from my desires.The preacher was in awe and asked the church to pray with me.

None of my coming home celebrations could compare to my life being saved by the grace of God. I was feeling powerful and could feel the change within me happening. I was walking different, talking different, I even drove different. I moved my seat up, no longer with a gangster lean to it. There were no ashtrays to empty, no newports or black and milds, I was clean of these things. There was no reason to feel uneasy because I wasn't hiding anything and God was in charge!

Our bible study began with a testimony service and I was sharing the beauty of when God pushed me up and out of my chair to the altar. Suddenly I felt a wave of excitement, a fresh wind which gave me new life and I had a new attitude about who I was. With butterflies in my stomach I was excited about a new beginning. Uncontrollably my tongue began to move, I was speaking in tongue as the spirit of God gave utterance; according to Acts 2: 2- 4. It was a beautiful experience to see how God was completely taking over my life and actually seeing the beauty in it.

With a new lease on life it seemed as if I'd share my story with whoever listened. I was in a happy place with my life. I was speaking with an elder and telling him about my the troublesome life I led. He was so impressed with my story that he was compelled to introduce me to Bishop Raul. Bishop Raul dissected me on the spot and got to the root of who I was destined to become. I was honest with him when asked what I wanted to be in life. I told him I always wanted to be like my uncle, Pastor Willie Calloway. I knew I couldn't be just like him because my life was so different. But the key to fulfilling your dream is staying focused on the finish line. The only thing that could stop me was me and I was getting out of my own way.

Bishop Raul wanted me to study with him and learn how to interpret and breakdown scriptures. He taught me how to enhance my gift and really invested in me. With a genuine smile he told me he saw a preacher. His eyes were sincere and he wanted to help me reach a higher level of ministry so much so that he was willing to work with me for free, which meant I was surpassing seminary school and studying theology. I was learning from the best, I was amazed at the doors that God was opening for me.

With these blessings I truly saw how people were affected in my receiving God's favor. My eyes were open to the envious way of family members and even church goers. However, I continued to push through and past these obstacles and remain focused on the goals set by myself and the Bishop. With all these blessings I managed to feel incomplete and reached out to someone who held a special place in my heart. I wanted to redeem myself with this young lady Trisha, she gave me a hard time due to my past but finally agreed to meet with me. Over dinner at Applebee's Trisha and I began our courtship.

With Trisha and I becoming close once again, and my life taking a new path I sat with my mentor, my grandmother. My grandmother advised me to fast, pray on it and to make sure that she was the person for me. I'm sure that there were single pastors but I was determined to do the right thing and be like my uncle, Pastor Willie Calloway. I wanted to do the right thing by marrying Trisha. I was happy with her for the first few months, but sought spiritual counsel with God soon after. We found out we were expecting which was a surprise as she told me in the past, that she was unable to conceive. She was very sick during her pregnancy and our communication wasn't the best. I was becoming spiritually weak because she was not where I was. Her energy was draining me and I was getting out of character as we were not equally yoked. I was convinced that she was ready to be a housewife but her actions showed me otherwise. She really turned out to be a wolf in sheep's clothing.

I was a certified flagger and chose to work the night shift this was my way of avoiding the challenges of my marriage. With limited contact, Trisha and I really only saw one another Sundays at service. Although we weren't as close to one another, I was still very supportive of her during her pregnancy, I spoke to my son while he was in her womb. I focused on the baby and chose to ignore her childish antics for the betterment of our tattered relationship. My son DeLawrence decided to make an early entrance in the world, he was born in the 7th month. I was there for his birth and we tried to work it out but becoming a mother didn't mature her as I'd hoped.

Trisha and I tried but it was a lost cause and our marriage went downhill, I sought refuge on the sofa and she sought comfort in the arms of another. Trisha's dishonesty led to her being fired from work. With only one income in the household this caused tension between us. For six months I slept on the couch and cried out to God that "Not my will but thine will be done." There were nights she would come in at the wee hours of the the night or she wouldn't come home at all. As I felt my wife being pulled from me, I prayed for the exact type of woman I wanted. Someone that was cut out to be a first lady, one who could deal with people. I went to Unity Church of God and Christ, I needed God at that moment.

In my observance of the church and its members, I saw Jacqueline whom I'd seen over the years as our families are very familiar with one another. She made her way around the church to hug the woman directly right in front of me. At that moment I spotted Jacqueline, I realized she fit the exact description of the woman I asked God for. We greeted one another with a hug and I felt compelled to text her. I didn't know if I was right or wrong, but it was innocent. Through our text messages I shared with her that I was getting a divorce and was trying to cut cost. Surprisingly she was going through the same thing and offered to help me by printing the documents. My prayers were answered as Trisha's mom called the next day, she was irate and aggressive. She stated she was tired of my dealing with her daughter and that she would pay for the divorce herself!

Overtime I found myself becoming closer to Jackie, but I also saw her flaws which I thought would keep me from her. I thought she was a missionary, but when we hung out she smoked cigarettes, weed and she'd have a glass of wine. I confronted her about it and she said she liked who she was. She felt like I was trying to change her, she was cautious and had trust issues just like I did. However many issues presented themselves I remembered God's promise to me and I remained focused.

I realized how much social media particularly

Facebook played a part in our becoming closer and courting each other virtually. I was aware of where she was and she was aware of my moods and my current situations. I kept her informed of my divorce proceedings as she was adamant about not dating a married man. There were times I'd pop up on her unexpectedly due to a post she put up about the church events for the evening. I just wanted to be around her and she would do outlandish things to test me, one of them was taking me to see Kevin Hart.

A preacher at a Kevin Hart comedy show? I was so stiff and uncomfortable. This date was supposed to be casual, I didn't own any casual clothing. I was a suit man. I didn't know what to wear and even though I had a week's notice my schedule prevented me from planning my outfit a little better. At the last minute I asked my dad to come with me shopping. We wound up in Walmart, I bought some jeans, a sweater and some shoes that a put a hurting on my feet all night. On top of my discomfort for being at the show, my feet were barking consistently like a chihuahua at strangers. I did manage to laugh a little, but found myself concerned with the assumptions of people we knew and what they may have been thinking seeing me with Jackie.

Following our date at the Kevin Hart show, we went to Applebee's where I was more relaxed. My feet were still throbbing but since we were seated it didn't matter. I was more comfortable at

Applebee's. I was familiar with the staff as I was a regular there. Jackie and I laughed easily and conversed all night long, we closed the place. I felt better ending our night at Applebee's, I didn't feel convicted and my mind was in the right place. I had a chance to see a softer side of Jackie. I really liked what I saw.

8 CHAPTER EIGHT

He who finds a wife finds a good thing

Jacqueline Hicks started and ended my days, we'd be on the phone with one another from sun up to sundown throughout the day. She became my encouragement and I looked forward to hearing her voice more and more. I'd moved on from my marriage and was legally separated. I was now a roommate to my step dad, Andy in Renton Highlands. I was taking my time getting to know Jackie and found that I focused more on myself. I was trying to rebuild my finances and regrouping. I was still a certified Flagger and would work various shifts. I had a vehicle to get to and from but I needed my own place.

In evaluating my life and the plans I wanted to go forth with, I chose to fast and pray for two months. In this time I prayed for guidance and an opportunity for me to grow and lead others spiritually. My grandmother knew that I'd always had a passion for preaching and I'd asked about renting the basement to start my church. My grandfather told me I didn't have to rent the space because the upstairs would be free as their service ended earlier in the afternoon. With this opportunity I chose to focus on praying for God to guide me.

In my observance of my gift of preaching I found that some women were very aggressive and desperate. I found myself falling a little faster for Jackie than expected and I wanted to pump my brakes a little bit. I am a firm believer that men should pursue the women they're interested in and if the feeling is reciprocated the young lady should let that be known. But some of the women that I encountered were very aggressive and were determined to make themselves be more than what I may have seen in them. I did entertain one young lady but she couldn't hold my attention. I found myself wanting to talk to Jackie and see her more than anyone else. She was it, anyone else was invisible. She was becoming a key person in my life, a need which is something I have never felt for any woman.

I knew that Jackie was holding my heart in her hands when she took a trip to Las Vegas with her friends. During this trip it broke up our norm of speaking to one another consistently throughout the day. My ego wouldn't allow me to be as honest as I should have been and I became distant when she wouldn't answer my calls. I ignored her calls and found myself irritated when I couldn't speak to her when I wanted to speak with her. For the remainder of her trip I didn't communicate with her.

We didn't speak to one another until she came back from her trip with her friends. I poured my heart out to her and told her what I'd been through in my life with women. I proposed that if I wasn't loving her right that she should let me know because I needed to learn and grow from my past experiences. This talk allowed us to get closer with one another. However, we still had our challenges in trying to build a relationship.

Jackie brought me to her parents house for a visit and I met her parents formally. I'd seen them at church functions but now our meeting was more personal. I felt comfortable with my intention and asked for permission to date their daughter. I had to share my life story with them and her mother became nervous about my intentions with her daughter. Her dad was more lenient in offering me a chance. With one half the blessing Jackie and I officially began dating one another publically.

As a couple we went to church functions together and were inseparable. We hit a rock and a hard place with her birthday. Jackie still liked to party and would go out with her friends here and there. I was invited to come but declined because it wasn't a comfortable place for me. With her birthday coming up she wanted to go to a party and I flat out refused which caused a rift between us. We didn't speak for about a week which was difficult for both of us. Our separation didn't last long because we missed each other.

Smoking cigarettes, weed, drinking and partying were things that I could no longer be apart of. After a serious prayer session and fasting I asked God to show me if Jackie was supposed to be in my life because I wanted a saved woman and these behaviors she displayed were not that of a saved woman. Ironically the night before Jackie purchased Nicorette gum and the next day no longer had a desire to smoke. And slowly over time she no longer had no desire to smoke weed, drink or party.

I saw a complete change in Jackie within a matter of weeks, I knew that Ms. Jacqueline Hicks would be my wife. Seeing this miraculous change she made I could never doubt the power of God. I was strong in my belief, I showed discipline and I believe that my strength assisted in her changing for the better. I've learned that if you want to see change, you must first be the change. It definitely starts with you. Jackie confided in me that she had written down 32 characteristics that she wanted in a man and that I fit them all. I was both flattered and impressed that she'd written the blueprint for the man she wanted as I had prayed for the woman I wanted. The number one characteristic on her list was that I had to love God more than I loved her.

I went to visit my grandparents house and shared my intentions of marrying Jackie. Our families had been close with one another since the 50's and I told my granddad how much I wanted to marry Jackie. I didn't have as much money as I would have like to have had in efforts to provide for my future family. My grandparents loved Jackie and were very excited for me. My grandfather was as anxious as I was about my getting married to her. He even encouraged me to go to Las Vegas. He said they probably wouldn't care if we got married. But I couldn't move as fast as I would have liked because I still had a few weeks until my divorce was final.

Jackie and I regularly visited with her parents, we spent plenty of time over at their house. During a recent visit with her parents seated at the table I expressed myself and my intention to marry their daughter. I asked her dad for his daughter's hand in marriage, and her dad counseled me before answering. He kept inquiring about my recent divorce and whether or not I was ready to make such a commitment so soon after being divorced. They were honest about being very protective of Jackie due to her previous relationship and were weary of me and my intentions. Was I ready for Jackie? Was I ready to be married?

I explained that I was accustomed to having a woman by my side and I didn't feel complete without one. However, none of the previous women have made me feel as complete in comparison to Jackie. I was ready! With his blessing I began to make plans to make his daughter my wife. I still had a stash from my previous life and figured I would use this to purchase the ring for her. In getting an idea of her style of ring we went window shopping and we'd go in and out of jewelry shops. Seeing her style and what she liked I made my purchase and planned a night at Palisades, an upscale restaurant on the water. We were very elegantly dressed and turned heads as we made our way through the restaurant. I called ahead and informed them of my plans to propose and there was a dozen red roses beautifully arranged in a vase on our table.

We ordered appetizers and as she talked I became nervous, she was excited about the restaurant and chatted about its elegance. I was impressed with my surroundings as well but the proposal and her reaction superseded any other thoughts I may have had about the decor and elegance. Jackie was different from any other woman, with this thought in mind I was on my knee. When she realized what I was doing she screamed out in excitement!

"What are you doing? what are you doing?" Her eyes were huge in excitement.
"No you're not!" she squealed.

With her mouth hanging open anticipating my next move I took the box from my side pocket in my dinner jacket and opened it. The lighting was perfect as it bounced off of the 2ct princess cut yellow gold ring.

"Jackie, I love you and you know we've both been through it but I promised you that I wouldn't put you through anything like we've been through before. I love you and I would never put our relationship in any danger from any other woman or previous relationships with my children's mothers. I promise to be an amazing father to your son, Jackie. Will you marry me?" I asked.

"Yes! yes! I will!" her hands flew over her mouth in surprise and she started crying.

She hugged me with tears streaming down her face, I was so emotional and so happy with finding my partner for life. Jackie is right for me and I was so happy to have found her.

In typical couple fashion we posted pictures on Facebook of us at the Palisades restaurant and she named the photo album "I said, yes!" We had an overwhelming response of well wishes and congratulations. Our wedding was one month later on August 18, 2012 at my in-laws house, she was given away by her dad.

The blessings began to pour in immediately and I founded my own church on August 19, 2012. I was now in my uncle Willie Calloway's former church I decided to move forward with utilizing the space at the church. I'd asked my grandparents permission to use. The first service was amazing, my father-in-law spoke and the service was well attended. However the very next Sunday reality set in and they were only 10 of us, three of them were children. I was nervous about my future and whether or not I was really chosen to pastor. But I kept the faith and didn't waver. Jackie was encouraging and motivated me to keep moving in the direction that God had set out for me.

I never imagined that I would be a preacher with the way my life had gone for so many years. I never saw myself being successful especially as a pastor and I'm truly in awe of my life. I have changed completely. I thought my life was destined to forever be a gang member. But God knew different and having the wife I have, I'm truly grateful for a new start and truly having a friend in her. Our communication is stellar in comparison to many of the relationships I've tried in the past, my maturity and acceptance for a new life plays a big part in that.

9 CHAPTER NINE

(John 4:44). Christ also said 'no prophet is accepted in his hometown'.

Trials and tribulations will rock an unsteady foundation but when God sets it in place for you, there is nothing that you can't get through and past. With me upstarting the church and my grandmother's constant praising of how I reminded her of my uncle Pastor Willie when he preached, jealousy spread like wildfire. To my great dismay one afternoon there was a knock on my door and I was served, I was being sued! This lawsuit for using the church. My own family was suing me for $90,000! As the bible clearly states money is the root of all evil.

Members of my family, my cousins and my aunt were suing me for using the church, I couldn't believe it I was in shock. I was so hurt because here

I was trying to fix my life and take this path that God had for me. I had to know what was up so I reached out to my cousin after so much antagonizing. I called asked her to meet with me.

"Can I meet with you," I asked. She answered on the first ring.

"Sure," my cousin answered.

I had my wife accompany me to meet with my family, I relied on her support. Meeting with my cousin had somehow become awkward but it had to happen. I wasted no time asking questions.

"What do you have against me?" I asked, impatient with my arms crossed.

"I don't have anything against you but I don't understand how you went from zero to 100 overnight!" She stated with her hand on her hip.

"So you're telling me you don't believe in the power of God?" I asked, my eye widened.

"No I'm not saying that I'm just saying you were just in jail you were just a gang member and all of a sudden you're a pastor? I think there's a process." She stared back at me not backing down.

Needless to say I'd chosen to stay away from these members of my family. They came at me with everything they could think of to destroy my character, credibility, and my career. One Saturday afternoon I got a frantic phone call from a member of the choir we were locked out of the church! They changed the locks on me! The choir member tried to open the door for choir practice to find that his key didn't fit in the lock. I'm happy it wasn't on a Sunday it would have thrown us off completely.

We wound up spending $400 to have the locks changed. This propelled me to install cameras and they still broke in this time we were able to see that it was my family breaking into the church. I changed the locks again and had an ADT alarm system put in. Relentless in their fight for this property, they broke in again ignoring the blaring sound of the alarm and changed the locks once again. Upon the alarms going off at ADT the police were called to the church. Myself and a few members arrived at the same time of the police. When they were informed of it being a property dispute, they said we would have to go to court to settle the matter. After this information being shared, letters were sent to and from our attorneys and I was able to continue my services during the time of the lawsuit.

They were gathering an army to fight against my growth as a preacher. They were trying to turn so many people against me with the lawsuit, slander, lies, they tried to destroy my character. They referred to me as a flunky for serving the leaders. Before you can lead you have to know how to follow. In order to be the best leader I had to be the best follower. Even today my servant mentality gets me through, it reminded me of David who was tested and disrespected but had the makings of a king.

No matter how I tried to grow the immaturity and jealousy persisted to try my patience. While I was in St. Louis for a convention the efforts to make me backslide to "Too Sick," was still in effect. Text messages were sent to my wife as if I'd had an inappropriate conversation with my ex-wife. These messages were then posted on Facebook! I couldn't believe that all of these treacherous acts were because of money. I was completely disgusted. It was causing friction in my home.

My cousin Ebony was furious and took a closer look at the messages not believing that I'd do anything to ruin my life or my marriage. She compared my signature on my phone to the signature on the messages posted on facebook and found that my signature in messages coming from my phone were in a different font! I filed a petition of no contact order against my ex-wife for defamation of character and slander.

Being the pastor and having a first lady is similar to being a celebrity, you're expected to be perfect. No one is perfect and although people love you whether its gossip, blogs, newspapers or the news people are drawn to your imperfections. If you're not strong you will fall victim to your character being assassinated. You must protect yourself at all times, spiritual armour is a must. While people adore you on social media, you could easily become a meme, hot topic, or butt of someone's jokes. The same wonderful social media site that can propel you to the next level, can be the same that makes you want to hide under your bed. My being the victim of cyber bullying taught me alot about strength and being the bigger person, "Too Sick, and C Crazy," were not invited to this party. I had to deal with this issue mentally, this fight was different.

There was even an attempt to falsify documents and they had my grandmother taken off the board of directors! My own cousin who is a civil judge assisted in their winning the case against me. There was no money for them to win but they were awarded the church. I was disappointed at first because we spent so much money to repair and remodel the church. I had high hopes of being successful in that specific church because of its sentimental value to me. Their argument was that they were trying to maintain the legacy of my uncle Pastor Willie. But yet there was no evidence in that.

When I first got the church it had graffiti on the outside, there was no maintenance to the church. There was no pastor, there was 5 members in the church for years on end. There was no choir or musicians. It hurt me to see my uncle's legacy fall to the wayside. I felt it was my duty to take his legacy to the next level under a different name. We tried to share the space but it was hard to do this when there were petty acts such as tampering with the mixing board, it created a loud screeching noise when it was turned on, no heat, no air conditioner, no toilet tissue, and no soap. There was even a hitman sent in to hurt me, he came in with a black hoodie was threatening me and wouldn't budge.

I'd turned my cheek to my family during this trying time, and was at my wits end. I was not going to be disrespected in the house of God and I felt obligated as the shepherd to defend the sheep. I approached him and asked him to leave he said "no, you're not in charge!" I followed him outside and he charged me, I jumped in my boxing stance and once he saw that southpaw, he took off! I chased him all through the Central District. He started stripping and screaming through the streets "you see I'm crazy right? You see I'm crazy!"

My choir members were out there ready to take it to the streets while in the street. We wound up calling the cops.   My wife had been calling me the whole time "Pastor, Pastor!" I never heard her until she called me "Chris." I was so embarrassed and apologetic to my wife and my congregation for allowing myself to get so caught up in my anger nealy doing something I would regret. They were not receptive of my apology because they felt that I was right in protecting them from danger.

Anytime you're trying to do what's right you're going to be tested. But it's not about how you come out of your process that determines your future but how you go through the process because it can make you or break you. Although I was overwhelmed and hurt because I didn't understand how someone who loves you could hurt you and call themselves family. The same people were there to help me get out of trouble. But at this time it baffled me that my family was behaving this way. I refused to allow them to have me forfeit my future.

All these attacks on my life, career, my freedom, my marriage and I stood strong. With everything I faced I stayed strong. In this part of my life I feel as if my life compares to Job where everything was taken from me. Then everything came back to me because I became closer to God, stronger in my faith and secured in my future. Although I was strong and I made it through. There were times I struggled with who I am and who I was, the old me would have been brutal and vicious but the new me, this renewed man, faith filled man allowed God to handle my enemies. God's retaliation is much greater than my own and I had to realize that. When God retaliates it may not be at the time you want it to be. God is always on time and you must be patient and turn it over to him, trusting that it will be handled.

In my tests of faith, I've received so much flack for not being directly in the lives of my children, but when I have chosen to be a faithful man to my wife not everyone will want to respect my loyalty. I have spent the majority of my life behind bars due to lies and the spiteful ways of one of my sons mothers. My children are taken care of financially but I'm unable to see them due to the drama and immaturity I have to deal with.

I refused to deal with phone calls after 12AM, I refused to answer these phone calls. I wouldn't entertain visits after a certain time because it would have invited chaos and mayhem. There were sneaky acts of phone calls during the day when my wife was not at home. I had to put my wife in charge of communication with my children's mothers. This was a direct insult to any of them who may have had alternative plans for me personally. These things have categorized me as a deadbeat father.

One of the mothers had a live-in boyfriend, we had a good relationship in the beginning because she had a man. My son visited consistently and her and my wife got along easily. We were able to pick him up, and her and my wife used to talk on the phone all the time. As soon as the relationship between my sons mother and her boyfriend ended her disrespectful behavior began again. The calls at midnight, calling when my wife was at work. Not once did my faith waiver nor did I entertain the shenanigans.

One time in Applebee's my wife and I were eating and one of my children came into the restaurant to get my phone number. I have gone through enough with his mother to know that trouble would come from this. I refused to give my number as she would call at odd hours, hang up and prank call. I did ask for his phone number which he didn't know by memory. He went out to the car to get it from his mother, who decided to approach my table herself. She walked up to the table livid! With much attitude and her hair uncombed, her appearance unkempt. She was angry, loud and began to make a scene with her hand on her hip and rolling her head. She was inquiring about why I had something against her, I had nothing against her, I wasn't upset with her. I was too successful to be angry with her, I know my limits with you and there's too much negativity that came along with dealing with her. I used her approaching me at Applebee's as an example.

I understand the role and responsibilities of being of a father and I don't believe that that's the issue. The emotions I experience as a father are difficult, it's so easy to be called a deadbeat father. I know the drama I've dealt with in dealing with these women. I've seen the exchange between the women and my wife and the competition on their behalf. There is no competing with my wife, and there is no creating a wedge between us. With my daughter's mother, Jackie and I had a beautiful relationship, however I saw the tension slowly growing as I was growing as a preacher. The materialism increased and when I couldn't produce, my daughter was kept from me for at this time it's been 11 months.

I've learned to respect the classy and intelligent lady in my wife. My wife has a child from a previous relationship and her son has never been supported by his father. Jackie has never acted out with her son's father, never requested child support, she just moved on with her life. There are no pop ups or late phone calls. With the separation from me and my children, God lined me up with my family and I adopted my son, Freddy Boles. He's a great kid, straight A's, he wants to be a pastor like his dad and I am truly thankful for him. He's taught me so much, he's in Pilot school, he travels with us and he prays for me whenever he sees me down. I appreciate the beauty of fatherhood through my son Freddy Christopher Boles.

10 CHAPTER TEN

I'm so thankful to God that he turned my life around. I was recently asked again if I could change anything about my life what would I change... my response was nothing. If I didn't go through what I went through I wouldn't be prepared for today's time. My mother and grandmother's generations can't relate to the youth of today and the drugs they battle. I feel seasoned enough to deal with the children of this generation. I'm grateful for what I've encountered personally with relationships, and my incarcerations which taught me the value of real friendship. I now value my family, my wife, and people who really have my back.

There's been so many things throughout my life that I did where I was well off financially and today I have nothing to show for it. However, it all makes sense now because now I value everything I have.

Change presents itself but it's up to you to accept it. Without you accepting it, you continue on the same road until you accept change, until you say yes to change you'll never walk in change. I had to put my experiences behind me and speak life to myself. I had to say I'm better than the storm I'm in, I'm better than what I'm going through.

I didn't go through counseling, I didn't go to AA, or NA it took me speaking life to myself and declaring that I'm better than this. When I used to think about sitting in dope houses and selling dope I had to say to myself I'm better than this. I looked at the women I associated myself with and said I deserve better. I deserve more than just having kids. My destiny is greater than this. People have to understand that the key to change is accepting change. Move past your pride and accept change. Men have a macho ego, where we think we can do it on our own. But until you accept change you'll continue to be bound to your past.

In order for me to have had a good healthy relationship with my wife, I had to realize that it took God to push me into this situation. Out of all the people how could it be me that is so blessed to live the life I'm living. The people I've hurt, the lives I've taken how am I worthy? It kills me when people say "this is all I know." That isn't all you know you haven't been there all your life. There was a time you were loving and lovable. If people were to look past their pain they could go further in life. That's what I had to do.

I had to look past my pain and realize that just because my dad wasn't there didn't mean I couldn't be healed. Hurt can be healed. Healing is possible and so is forgiveness. I had to forgive myself for my sins, for hurting my family, for hurting families and for hurting myself. I had to forgive myself for the choices I made, for the repeated incidents and acts of violence that led me to the jail various times. Once I forgave myself I found myself surrounded with people that I would have never been in the same room with willingly.

I would have never been in the same room with Police Chiefs working side by side with them to heal the youth in hopes of having them choose a better life. I'm currently sitting on the Task Force Board in working with underprivileged youth. There is a judge I actually work with as she sits on a board for Youth Link and we work side by side to help underprivileged youth in our area. They rely on me and support me in my efforts. They don't allow my past to dictate my future. It's such a blessing to have turned my life around and it took so many steps for me to get here. Loving myself and understanding myself. You have to understand your weaknesses and your strengths before you could move past your pain. If not you'll be held hostage to your past.

I thought change would be hard but the more you go

through, the stronger your faith becomes you depend more on God because you can't do it by yourself. And once you move *self* out of the way you can go much further in life. You realize that it's going to take God and it was no one but God that blessed me with the wife I have, the job, my looks, my car it was God. I find Mark 10:9 to be so true, what therefore God hath joined together, let not man put asunder. Ever since I held Jesus by his promise and by his word he's never failed me.

One thing I learned about this process is that it caused me to be more isolated and private. Our relationship is now more private. Due to reactions of people we know we are not as affectionate on social media. Our posts or pictures have always been tasteful but somehow ruffled the feathers of some. Showing love as Barack Obama did for his first lady Michelle is the same way I love and admire Jackie publicly. In celebration of love and great partnership and pushing this idea more on our youth as opposed to a love them and leave them mind set. Respect them and keep them, Will Smith and Jada, Jay z and Beyonce, Denzel and Pauletta, find a Queen or King and build with her, support will take you places beyond your imagination.

My thoughts were interrupted by a knock on my office door, the congregation was ready and waiting for my sermon. My assistants came into the office and prayed with me in preparation to address the congregation. They are by my side as I greet people on the way to the pulpit. As I sat waiting for the choir to finish the song I mentally prepare to address the church. I am joy filled to see a full house on this Sunday. I approach the pulpit and I take into consideration what was just sung **"He's able"** and as I refer to my text. My motto is "I preach for results and not response." To see men and women, boys and girls come to the altar crying out "What must I do to be saved." It's been worth the journey.

LETTER FROM MOM

Dear Chris,

I remember when you were about 12 years old, you wanted to stay with your dad and I didn't allow you to do so because you were *my* baby. I was very protective of you. Your oldest sister   was grandma and grandpa's baby, but you were mine and I raised you myself. I didn't want to share you. When you started acting out and was placed in a smaller classroom setting, I was called constantly to the school because the teachers had so many issues with you being disruptive. My faith never wavered but I surely grew weary.

There are no instructions that come with children but there were times I wish there were. The times I had to visit you in King County were the worst. I would be hysterical after every visit when I had to leave you there. Visiting you was so hard but when the news came on and a horrible crime was committed I was relieved that you were in there and it wasn't you they were talking about. There were times I couldn't imagine what you may have been going through while you were locked up. I had no idea that you were fine and very capable of handling yourself. I would get so depressed when you were in and out of jail, I even contemplated suicide a few times. If it weren't for my parents I could have easily been a drug addict or an alcoholic.

There were times I passed you on the street because I couldn't even speak to you. It was even hard to be around children. I'd always heard that children were a blessing but I couldn't see the blessing. It was very hard to be a single parent and when things were rough it felt as if you three would never grow up. But, when you are finished going through, you do make it. Everything I went through made me stronger as a woman and as a parent. It helped me to be able to deal with life. I am so proud of the man you've become I'm completely in awe.

I find myself calling *you* for wisdom, you have more wisdom than I have. I now run things by you just to get your perspective. The way you think is mind blowing. To see you as you are now, I am very proud. I look forward to Sundays to hear you preach. Every Sunday I learn something new without fail. I'm simply in awe of you, my son. I always say I can't believe *all of that came out of me*, it's hard to believe.

I love you so much Chris, and I'm so proud to be your mother.

All my love,

Mom

Pastor Lawrence Christopher Boles, III
The Man, The Ministry, The Mission

Pastor Lawrence Christopher Boles, III, prophetically preaches with precision, passion, and power. He is a man after God's own heart, with a heart for the people of God. Anointed and appointed for such a time as these.

Pastor Boles was born on January 5, 1980 in Renton, Washington. He grew up at Bethany Temple Pentecostal Church, where his uncle the late Rev. Willie Calloway was the Pastor and Founder. It was during his formative years as a young man that he acknowledged the call of God on his life to preach the Gospel. He was saved and baptized with the Holy Ghost at the age of 14, but drifted away from God in his later teens. However, what the enemy meant for bad, God turned it around for good! In 2008 Pastor Boles surrendered and gave his life back to Christ.

The Lord has given Pastor Boles a dynamic testimony, from the prison to the pulpit. Where he was facing a sentence of 42 years, but because of the favor of God upon his life, he only served 6 years. Pastor Boles shares his testimony of restoration and reconciliation across the Nation, not just in the pulpit but also in the same streets the Lord delivered him from. As a result; gang members, drug dealers, and misguided men and women of all ages have given their lives to Christ.

Pastor Boles is the proud father of 6 beautiful children. In 2011, after seeking the Lord for a virtuous woman, the Lord sent the love of his life, Lady Jacqualine S. Hicks. They married on August 18, 2012, and together birthed and established Redeemed by the Blood Pentecostal Church on August 19, 2012. In March 2017, Redeemed by the Blood became one church in two locations (Kent and Lynnwood, WA) better known as their North & South Campus. Since the inception of Redeemed by the Blood, many souls have been saved, healed, delivered, and set free.

As a member of the Church of God in Christ, Inc. Pastor Boles serves in official capacities of leadership within the District, Jurisdiction and on a Regional level:

- District Chairman, L.J. Green District

- Episcopal Adjutant, to the presiding prelate of the WA Northwest Ecclesiastical Jurisdiction.

- President, Department of Evangelism, WA Northwest Ecclesiastical Jurisdiction.

- President, Region 6 (Alaska, Idaho, Oregon and Washington) Church Of God In Christ Inc.

- Special Assistant to the President of the North West Regional Youth department Church of God In Christ Inc.

- International Evangelist of the Church of God In Christ

In 2017, Pastor Boles founded the Team Redeemed Life Center, he serves as Executive Director of this community based program that supports local police departments and other law enforcement agencies in conducting educational outreach activities in the City of Kent, for at risk youths and teens involved in gang-related activities.

Pastor Boles has a sincere and earnest desire to reach the lost at any cost, to advance and expand God's Kingdom. Whether preaching as Pastor on a Sunday morning, or ministering as a traveling Evangelist, or witnessing beyond the four walls of the Church, the Anointing of God is evident and prevalent on this man of God's life.

Made in the USA
Monee, IL
22 July 2020